Legalizing Illegal Aliens Via Resident Visas

A great Americans-first plan which saves $Trillions. Learn how!

Countries as far away as Australia have problems with migrants taking native jobs. They use a technique called the Assisted Voluntary Return as part of an overall Pay-to-Go plan to incent migrants to leave Australia and return back home. Pay-to-Go across the world pays both travel expenses and offers a generous stipend for those who sign up for the offer to return home.

But, what about those who would not leave the USA no matter what the incentive? Are we better off with the remainder of 60 million illegal interlopers staying in the shadows of America, rather than devising a plan to solve the problem in a way that keeps America whole and makes Americans masters of our own country again?

The last official try by eight corrupt US Senators was called the Gang-of-Eight plan and it basically gave up America and Americans for the benefit of the illegal interlopers. It put them on a fast track to citizenship that would cost US taxpayers up to $6.3 Trillion with all of its provisions. In 2013, Americans told Congress and the House voted "no" and we sent the Gang of Eight Senators packing.

Unfortunately, if we do nothing to end the tremendous cost and sacrifice of accommodating the 60 million illegal interlopers in the shadows of the USA, we cannot sustain our resolve. Will the gang of 8 re-emerge and take us down? How long can we Americans withstand this situation, which many rightfully call *A Mexican Standoff*. Our country is clearly in chaos; a race to the bottom in wages is underway; and regular Americans are losing the jobs and low-wages war every day.

Meanwhile, there is no American consensus as Democrat-dominated American cities and certain Democrat states decided to offer sanctuary to illegal foreigners rather than supporting the needs of American citizens. The point is that if we opt to do nothing, this real standoff in the USA is scheduled never to end.

The one clear choice for those wishing to stay in America would be if we can legalize interlopers with no benefits. This would end the sanctuaries and the shadows and be good for everybody. I think we can do it.

In this book, you can read about how to legalize Illegal Aliens Via Resident Visas. It takes interlopers out of the shadows and gives them the opportunity they seek while keeping Americans whole and keeping the country prospering. You're going to like this America-first plan built by an American for Americans.

BY

Brian W. Kelly

LETS GO PUBLISH

AF797725

Title: **Legalizing Illegal Aliens Via Resident Visas**
Copyright © 2017 Brian W. Kelly
Publisher: Brian P. Kelly
Author Brian W. Kelly

Published by: LETS GO PUBLISH!
Editor Brian P. Kelly
Email: info@letsgopublish.com
Web site www.letsgopublish.com

Library of Congress Copyright Information Pending

Book Cover Design Brian W. Kelly
Publisher Brian P. Kelly

ISBN Information: The International Standard Book Number (ISBN) is a unique machine-readable identification number, which marks any book unmistakably. The ISBN is the clear standard in the book industry. 159 countries and territories are officially ISBN members. The Official ISBN For this book **978-1-947402-17-1**

The price for this work is: **$12.95 USD**

10 9 8 7 6 5 4 3 2 1

Release Date: November 2017

LETS GO PUBLISH!

Dedication

I still have not gotten over losing my dog Ben, last Thanksgiving. He sure enjoyed himself on the day he moved on. He would not have permitted us to change any of his great remembrances as the Thanksgiving Turkey carving time for all his years, was one of Ben's favorites.

Each & Every day before this year 2017 or so it seems, when I would go to work in the front office, and sometimes even before I would arrive, my two co-workers on every other book project were there to greet me and work with me all day—other than for extremely necessary bio-breaks for all parties.

This book is dedicated to these two fine individuals
Benny, the first little man below, passed away on Thanksgiving last year after a fine stuffest; but his spirit continues with me.
Buddy does his best to make up for Ben's absence. And I love the little guy for his wonderful acceptance of the loss of his best dog friend in life

Ben *& Dad*

Buddy*, Ben & Mom*

Acknowledgments:

I appreciate all the help that I have received in putting this book together as well as all the other 131 books from the past.

My acknowledgments were so large at one time that readers complained that they had to go through too many pages to get to page one of the book.

And, so in response, I put my acknowledgment list online, and it continues to grow. Believe it or not, it costs about a dollar less to print my books today than then. No kidding!

Thank you, my dear friends and supporters of many years. May God bless you all for your help.

You may check out www.letsgopublish.com to read the latest version of my heartfelt acknowledgments updated for this book.

A new lover of literature, Wily Ky Eyely continues her supportive efforts.

Thank you all very much!

Brian

Preface:

What would you call a plan that solved a problem for America that most of the Congress seems to have no interest in solving? I have called it many things while perfecting this book, but now let me settle my mental rumblings with what it should be called *The Resident Visa Plan*. It has a companion plan called the *Pay-to-Go Plan*.

This book, *Legalizing Illegal Aliens Via Resident Visas* is the second book of two which fully address the solution to 60 million interlopers residing in America. The first book, which was released several weeks ago is the companion book. Its title is Pay-To-Go. Both of these books should be required reading for every House and Senate member as well as the President of the United States. This is the only plan that can work for Americans first to end the shadows and the sanctuaries and save America about a $Trillion per year. Both books are available on the Amazon and Barnes & Noble sites.

The Resident Visa Plan is a vision for a secret sauce solution to fix the problem of 60 million interlopers waking up in America every day without our permission. Yes—build the wall, please! But simultaneously solve the residence problem of so many people who do not belong here in America. Do we really need up to 60 million interlopers in residence? I do not think so. Hey, John McCain thinks there are over 128 million interlopers in residence. Maybe he is right. Do we need 128 Million? Can anybody tell me what we need? My personal thoughts say we need zero. It is time to give Americans an opportunity to work in America.

I am very pleased that you are reading this book and I hope many others find it and convince the US Administration and the Congress and the President that it is their turn to learn about The Resident Visa Plan. It should have been obvious without me, a guy from no place giving Congress and the President a good idea.

The Resident Visa solution is unique and everything needed to implement it is already in place. It directly addresses the issues that having 60 million illegal foreign nationals in residence have brought upon America. Nobody likes deportation but just like you would throw an uninvited guest out of your house, it would be very fair for the US to throw out (deport) the 60 million uninvited guests in America today.

Yes, deportation is fair of course as these folks have broken our laws. But, our politicians are culpable as they made it too easy for foreigners to break our laws. The problem is that we do not see them in our house every day and so most of us have no stomach for deporting them.

Therefore, an adjunct solution to the Resident Visa Plan is a Pay-to-Go Plan. The US will pay the return expenses for each illegal interloper who chooses to return to their home country. Moreover, depending on their status in the USA, the government will provide a generous stipend of anywhere from $20,000 to $50,000 once they return. That's a good deal.

Amnesty is not a solution as Americans have already paid a big price for the largesse of politicians wanting low wages and those wanting the future votes of today's interlopers.

Ideally, the solution would be to go poof, and every foreign interloper would be taken back to where and when they crossed the border years and years ago.

Every plan requires fine tuning and we would expect this to continue to be the case with the Resident Visa Plan. When illegal interlopers do not want to be paid to go, and they want to stay in the US, the Resident Visa Plan comes in very handy. Together these plans are the long-sought solution to 60 million illegals in America. Nobody will be illegal and there will be no need for sanctuary citizens.

A key element of this plan is that each year the clock resets on foreign nationals who are permitted here on a temporary basis under the Resident Visa Plan. This book, thus focuses on interlopers signing up to become Resident Visa Holders with appropriate renewal assurances for good behavior.

In summary, this book presents the Resident Visa Plan as the fix and the Pay-to-Go Plan as the backup fix. Then it offers many other points on why this is the one and only fix to create an America without shadows that favors Americans 100%. There is so much good left over that good-willed interlopers have a lot to gain simply by signing up.

You are going to love this book as well as the plans themselves. All interlopers immediately are to be registered and accountable. You will see that The Resident Visa Plan is designed by an American for Americans.

Additionally, illegal foreign nationals will be very pleased because the plan uses deportation as a very last resort and it immediately gets illegal foreign nationals out of the shadows. Few books are a must-read but The Resident Visa Plan will quickly appear at the top of America's most read list.

This is a simple, America-first solution but only if Congress and the President have the guts! It solves the problem with 60 million interlopers in America and many others!

Table of Contents

About the Author

Brian W. Kelly retired as an Assistant Professor in the Business Information Technology (BIT) program at Marywood University, where he also served as the IBM i and midrange systems technical advisor to the IT Faculty. Kelly has designed, developed, and taught many college and professional courses. He is also a contributing technical editor to a number of IT industry magazines, including "The Four Hundred" and "Four Hundred Guru" published by IT Jungle.

Kelly is a former IBM Senior Systems Engineer and he was a candidate for US Congress from Pennsylvania. He has an active information technology consultancy. He is the author of 131 other books, in many topical areas, as well as hundreds of articles. Kelly has been a frequent speaker at many US conferences. Invite him to your next conference on immigration solutions.

When Brian ran for Congress as a Democrat against a 13-term Democrat in 2010, he took no campaign contributions, spent just enough to buy signs and T-shirts, and as a virtual unknown. Yet, he captured 17% of the vote. Kelly says: "Writing books is lots easier than running for public office!"

Chapter 1 Is There a Solution?

60 million interlopers cost many taxpayer dollars

If we knew how to immediately stop the drain on our government treasury with one bold and very fair move, would America's inept politicians make that move? I have done many analyses and I have concluded that American politicians, from Congress and the Senate on down. will never support Americans unless convinced that they would be out of office otherwise.

Based on what it costs to support illegal foreign nationals (average of $30,000 per person per year), the US can certainly afford to deport millions of people. But, the dirty politicians and the corrupt press preach a different mantra that puts Americans last and illegal aliens first.

Ironically, though Americans complain about all of the illegal aliens, supporting them, having them take their jobs, and lowering the average wages in America, most would prefer a different solution than rounding them up and deporting 60 million people. But, we can afford deportation if we choose. If nobody was collecting welfare, this would be a lot tougher, and if nobody in illegal status was stealing from Americans, maybe no American would care.

Can we afford a mass deportation of illegal foreign nationals—even without a roundup?

Is there a consensus for or against the idea? It only matters if the US can actually afford to undertake a mass deportation?

Let me prove that we can afford deportation before we move on to solutions that we can stomach. I am not recommending mass deportation but we can certainly afford it and the US can save lots of money if we chose to do it.

Let's say that 30 million of the 60 million illegal aliens in residence collect some form of welfare from the US to help afford their lives in America. What does that cost us per year?

The cost per year is $30,000 X 30,000,000 = $900 Billion per year
The cost of deportation is $10,000 X 30 million = $300 Billion one time

The first-year savings is a net of $600 Billion after deportation. The second and subsequent years, the savings would be the full $900 Billion per year

Rather than look at the unpleasant task of coerced deportation, many countries across the world have instituted what they call *Pay-to-Go* programs in which a free return and a stipend incentive are offered to the migrants to induce them to return home. In our country we would be incenting illegal interlopers living in the shadows of America.

A very nice stipend amount that would persuade many interlopers to return to their home country is $20,000. In this way, the deportation is really a voluntary emigration back to the home country.

The cost of the stipend at $20,000 X 30,000,000 = $600 Billion one time. This is if the country is the USA.

In this example, the cost of the return and the cost of the stipend would be $900 billion if every interloper agreed to return home and then executed on their promise.

This is the same amount as the cost to support an interloper in the US for one year. The difference between the two is the savings. In year 1, in this scenario, the savings would be zero dollars and the cost would be zero dollars. In year two an annual savings of $900 billion would begin to accrue. Where does the savings come from? It comes from the US not having to pay welfare to illegals as well as Americans being able to get jobs that pay substantially more than when the interlopers were depressing wages by accepting sub-minimum wage positions. .

Suppose the Pay-to-Go stipend were raised to $50,000, to attract more takers, the annual savings of as much as $900 billion would begin to accrue in year three so the stipend could be paid for. After year three, the US is in the black on the program.

Talk to your Congress

I predict that the biggest obstacle in solving the problem of 60 million illegal interlopers in America will be both chambers of the US Congress. I am not naïve enough to suggest that the current Congress' predilection for more voters and lower wages for all Americans could be overcome by the fact that this plan to deal with resident interlopers is the best yet conceived. So, if they remain recalcitrant, we may be forced to replace the entire Congress in order to do the right thing for America.

John McCain is known for his personal estimate of about 4 million per year jumping the border. He is talking about Illegal aliens, which we like to refer to as illegal interlopers. An interloper is another word for an uninvited guest.

McCain's estimate is of those who have chosen to cross the southern border. In his estimate, he does not include the million or more a year who simply decide not to go home when their visas expire. Instead they opt for illegal residency in the US. That's how we got into this problem in the first place. We did not invite 60 million people to America to sponge off US taxpayers. However, some of our elite representatives may very well have done exactly that.

US. amnesty advocate John McCain, is a recognized authority on the subject of illegal immigration. In a letter dated February 2004, he wrote that apprehension figures demonstrated that "almost four million people crossed the US border illegally in 2002."

McCain estimates over 10,000 cross every day. If it were exactly 10,000, then 3,650,000 per year would be his estimate. Instead he simply rounded it up to 4 million. That comes to 128 million from 1986, the year of the Reagan amnesty to the end of 2017. If we cut that in half and round it down, we're looking at my long-time estimate of 60 million interlopers in residence today. I know that nobody can prove me wrong on that number.

The purpose of this book is to find a solution to the big problem of having 60 million illegal interlopers (uninvited guests) permanently enshrined in an illegal status in the United States today. There are three International plans implemented in a number of countries such as Australia to help migrants(illegal aliens in our US situation) return to their home countries. They are as follows:

1. Assisted Voluntary Return (AVR)
2. Assisted Voluntary Return & Reintegration (AVRR)
3. Pay-to-Go

The plans are self-descriptive. AVRR programs work with the governments in the home country so that after the return, the migrant can reintegrate with society in his or her country. This is a great idea. Pay-To-Go encompasses any plan that pays anything such as transportation costs home, reintegration costs, and/or stipends to induce interlopers or migrants to choose to return home.

There is no question that incenting a mass exodus from a country overcrowded with non-citizen migrants, legal or illegal, without the need for deportation can be a very effective way to again gain control of the illegal immigration situation in the United States.

In our country. I would recommend that the US implement a comprehensive Pay-to-Go program as soon as possible. Otherwise, the raw numbers of interlopers that are increasing every year will eventually bankrupt the US.

Generally, a citizen of a foreign country who wishes to enter the United States must first obtain a visa, either a nonimmigrant visa for temporary stay, or an immigrant visa for permanent residence. For the most part, immigrant visas that are approved for permanent residence result in green cards.

Temporary visas for travel are easy to get. In 2016, well over 10 million such visas were issued. In 2017, it is expected that there will be 11 million temporary visas issued. Since many countries are not required to produce visas, the numbers coming in are substantially higher, more like 60 to 70 million passports needing no visas.

What about legal immigration?

About 1.2 million green cards are expected to be issued in 2017. In 2014, a total of 1,016,518 persons became lawful permanent residents aka, LPRs complete with green card status. Over half of the new LPRs (53 percent) already lived in the United States when they were granted lawful permanent residence. Sixty-four percent of the new LPRs were granted lawful permanent resident status based on a family relationship with a U.S. citizen or lawful permanent resident of the United States. The leading countries of birth of new LPRs were Mexico (13 percent), India (7.7 percent), and China (7.5 percent)

The other type of legal resident in the US is known as a birthright citizen, colloquially known as an anchor baby.

If the stipend is a little higher, the Pay-to-Go Program could save the US another ton of funds if it were also used to attract green card holders on welfare, and anchor babies on welfare. When and if they agreed to return to their home countries there would no longer be a cost for their welfare. Think of what the US could do with another half trillion or as much as a full trillion dollars per year to spend on American interests?

The three categories for which the program could be used to include would be the following:

1. Current interlopers
2. Legal green card holders on welfare
3. Anchor babies at any age, including children supervised by a legal or illegal parent.

The recommended stipend for each of the three categories would be as follows:

1. Current Interlopers	$20,000
2. Legal Green Card Holders on Welfare	$30,000
3. Anchor Babies or Adults	$50,000

Anybody opting for a stipend in any of the above categories would be prohibited without special petition from ever returning to the United States for any reason. Any debt accrued that is accounted for in the Accountability system, explained in Chapter 17. would need to be collected prior to any request for readmission to be examined.

There are 15 million legal immigrants (green card holders) currently in the country. Half of them are on welfare. 7.5 million X $30,000 = $225 Billion per year.

There are 6 million birthright citizens (former anchor babies) born to illegal aliens currently in the country. They are almost all on welfare 6 million X $30,000 = $180 Billion per year

The US can thus save an additional $405 Billion per year by adding the above two categories to the illegal interlopers able to use the Pay-to Go program or any other program that reduces costs to zero. This would make a total of three categories for which the program could be used.

What problem does the Pay-to Go program fix? It is a pro-America and pro-American citizen solution. It is an America-First solution to the major problem of 60 million illegal residents sponging off the taxpayers in the United States.

Once in the continental US, the interlopers either wholly or partially depend on US taxpayer dollars for their daily sustenance. Is your wallet looking a little thinner these days? The problem we plan to solve in this book, *the real problem,* is that 60 million illegal foreign nationals cost Americans money every day. They just don't pay their way and live here. They take from US.

Chapter 2 Should We Send 60 Million Back Home?

Maybe!!!

Maybe we should send them back if that is what they want. It is my contention that we lured them into America by giving them the idea that the streets were paved with gold and when they took their share of that gold, the streets would grow more gold. They are culpable for sure but our politicians deceived them by not building a wall and by not enforcing our border protections.

Because of the role of corrupt American politicians in their coming here, there was an implicit promise that illegal interlopers could stay and we Americans would make sure that they were OK. Because of America's role in bringing them here, I would say that we owe them at least a free trip home with a little pocket money. But, we can afford a lot more and it would serve us well if we paid it.

Yes, you heard me right. We need to pay for their return 100% and give them some pocket money. We already estimated the cost to taxpayers in this chapter of a full-boat fake-id welfare recipient in 2017 at about $30,000 per year. We also calculated the savings of giving interlopers, green card holders, and anchor babies a large sum to go home. If the US were a business, it would be very prudent to institute a Pay-to-Go program.

I have written a complete book titled *Pay-to-Go*, available on Amazon that explores all of the details of the proposed US *Pay-to-Go* program. It is a great program and the US can afford it and it would benefit all Americans. Feel free to read the Pay-to-Go book for more information.

Both the Pay-to-Go and another program which we are about to discuss must be instituted together in the US for us to solve the problem of 60 million interlopers in residence in the shadows of America.

The fact is that not everybody will be willing to leave and return even though they would be returning to their homes.

Chapter 3 What If An Interloper Does Not Want to Return Home?

Can anything be less appealing than the shadows?

A reasonable estimate is that with a $20,000 stipend, between 20% and 50% of the 60 million illegal aliens residing in America would take the money and return to their homes. Why would they want to persist in the shadows living in squalor, when they could get a great start with a big hunk of money back in their own country?

What we as a country would not want if we put forth a program to solve the problem is for just 20% of the problem to be solved. We might have 80% of the illegal residents remaining in the shadows. Then what? Would we even notice the improvement?

If illegal interlopers choose to stay in America, we have to make that OK or we wind up like today with shadows, sanctuary cities, and too many bad guys with a place to hide. However, the terms must favor Americans. To get out of the shadows, any illegal interloper would be required to agree to those terms.

The US savings on the Pay-to-Go as we proved is huge and it is easy to calculate. After the first year it is $30,000 per alien who returns per year. Not having to pay $30,000 per illegal alien is like making $30,000 extra. Over a lifetime, that would save taxpayers $1.8 million per person. Multiply $30,000 by 60,000,000 by 60 years to get $108 trillion in total possible savings? How can Congress say no?

Now what if we let them stay here legally rather than in sanctuary cities and in the shadows? How would that be good for Americans? The Resident Visa program is designed for an America-first country. It can produce the same savings one year sooner than Pay-to-Go as there is no cost at all for this program. All program costs are paid by the resident visa holders. I am sure you want to hear more about this

I don't want to go home, period!

If a resident illegal foreign national really does not want to go home and would rather live in the shadows or in sanctuary in Chicago, regardless of the cash incentive to return home, should Americans simply accept that as the end of negotiations? Without another program that fits, we would continue to be stuck in America with shadows and an underground economy, and a ton of illegal interlopers tapping the welfare system with fake stolen identification—perhaps using your social security number.

Desperate people do desperate things. Who wants 60 million desperate people living next door? Nobody in America would think the problem is solved if that is all that remains from the Pay-to-Go proposition.

There is no amnesty in this deal

There is always another option. This one actually costs US taxpayers nothing and it permits the interloper who will not go home, to stay in America indefinitely in a temporary legal status as long as they "behave." The big differences between this and the shadows and sanctuary cities is that the shadows and sanctuaries are completely gone and will be illegal.

The big difference between this and amnesty is that there is no welfare for Resident Visa Holders, and there is no green card to make the visa holder a permanent resident on a path to citizenship. They are temporary visa holders and that is it. They are not half-citizens or semi-citizens or legal permanent residents or citizens. They are simply holders of a legal visa in the US. They have the same rights as any other temporary visa holder plus one more.

Each year, they can renew their temporary Resident Visa by paying a renewal fee and being vetted again. The former illegal interlopers become legal temporary residents with a $100 to $200 annual renewal depending on what is cost effective for Americans.

From a financial standpoint, each former interloper, in order to gain the benefits of no-shadows, must agree to participate in zero welfare programs. If the illegal interlopers cannot afford the financial demands of the Resident Visa program after ten years, they would still be able to participate in the Pay-to-Go program. They could return home voluntarily with a large stipend. New illegal aliens who break-in after the inception of the program would be deported immediately.

As a big benefit for Americans, the shadows and the sanctuaries would be gone completely. Ever former aliens would be registered in the system once they get their special passport. US authorities would know how many there are and know for sure who they are. Multiply the number of illegal interlopers left after the completion of the Pay-to-Go program by the $30,000 per person per year savings to calculate the annual savings for this resident program.

Since this system depends on working computer systems, we can use the same system for other visa holders so that they cannot get lost when their visas expire.

The US Immigration Department already issues millions of travel visas for potential interlopers from other countries on a temporary basis and they have a cost of about $140.

The US would need to assure that a system would be in place that would permit a one-year expiration on a Resident Visa and an option for an annual renewal for all 60,000,000 interlopers left behind after Pay-to-Go. If there is no renewal, deportation or coerced Pay-to-Go at the lowest stipend rate become the only options left.

After each year, the resident visa holder would be able to renew the Resident Visa for another year unless they have broken the terms of the arrangement. They will never vote and they will never cost the US a dime. And, they can never commit a crime.

So, what I am proposing is that the program provides for granting interlopers in good standing what we should simply call a *Resident*

Visa. This would be a new visa type that, unlike other visa types can be renewed each and every year with conditions.

With this, former illegal foreign nationals would be legalized under the protection of the Resident Visa. They could remain in America out of the shadows on a one-year renewable temporary basis as long as they behaved in a lawful manner according to the exact terms of their visa.

There are many differences between illegally gaining benefits in the United States and becoming legal by gaining a Resident Visa. Those choosing to employ the Resident Visa to stay in America, are welcome to do so for one year after the program begins. However, the terms of the relationship with US officials will not be the same as when they were illegal. No illegal aliens will be tolerated one year after the program commences. Additionally, after one-year, the illegal interlopers who do not obtain their visa, would have the option of coerced deportation or Pay-to-Go.

There will be a vetting process in order to initially be approved. The visa will be special in that it will be renewable with a fee of $100 to $200, required annually after a renewal application, a record update (demographics, etc.), and a re-vetting of the applicant, and an eventual special oath of allegiance.

There are major benefits to the former foreign national for going through this process. The Resident Visa holder will receive an official photo ID at their application source so they do not have to carry a passport or an accompanying visa.

For those familiar with the notion of American visas, this unique visa would permit those approved, to live in America as long as they want, on a temporary but renewable basis for as long as they want as long as they renew their Resident Visa each and every year.

In essence, this process provides a Resident Visa, which would be an official US visa. Like all other US Visas, this would provide all of the benefits of a US non-immigrant category visa and more.

Will the press represent this program properly?

Members of the liberal progressive ideology, including over 90% of the media, have a habit of taking words and making their usage appear to be, for want of better words, dissatisfactory and disrespectful. There is nothing intrinsically wrong with the word illegal, and there is nothing intrinsically wrong with the word, alien.

Moreover, when the term illegal alien, as used in US immigration law, is used in everyday speech, there is nothing implied that makes the term disrespectful to the person who fits the description. It is merely a statement of fact that permits an individual to be identified and described with accuracy without caring about their name.

What types of US Visas are there?

The type of visa that a visitor or traveler must obtain is defined by U.S. immigration law, and relates to the purpose of the travel. There is one new category of visa proposed for current illegal alien US residents in addition to the two main categories in existing U.S. law:

1. **Nonimmigrant visas**– For travel to the USA on a temporary basis.
2. **Immigrant visas**–For travel to live permanently in the United States.
3. **Resident visas**–*New*--For current resident aliens to live temporarily in the US on a temporary but annually renewable basis.

Description of the new visa category

Under the new Resident Visa Program, a third type of visa would be authorized by US officials. It would be called a *Resident Visa*. Current law says all visa holders must first have passports containing information such as their home country and other pertinent information. The new visa category will also require a passport.

The new visa category is intended for those residents formerly in an illegal status, who register for and are granted a Resident Visa. Unlike other visas, the Resident Visa may be renewed annually as long as the holder does not violate the terms of the visa.

Like all visa requests, the individual must first possess a passport and then apply for the Resident Visa. The costs for the resident passport and the Resident Visa would be the same as under current law. An additional charge may be added to the visa fee for an ID card so the Resident Visa holder does not have to keep the passport and visa on their person at all times.

The visa is renewable annually for a $100 to $200 fee to reflect changes such as address or marital status etc. The ID card and picture must be refreshed at least every five years.

If we include the *Pay-to-Go* program, the new program in its entirety, would provide for the voluntary egress (with stipend) of illegal aliens as well as providing Resident Visas for those who choose to stay. An interloper would get to execute just one of these options. If the program were fully adopted by US officials as law or as an Executive Order, a proper name would be *Pay-to-Go* for one type of solution or and the other solution would best be named as the *Resident Visa* Program.

The most important part of this action if taken by Congress that most Americans would want to learn to assure that they are getting a fair shake from the government is the Resident Visa Program. In this case the former interlopers are being legalized on a temporary basis and will continue to live among Americans.

The Pay-to-Go is fairly self-explanatory. My opinion is that it will remain the quiet part of this complete revolutionary program. Despite its serendipitous presence, it is such a great deal for both parties that it has the potential to save the US the most treasury tax dollars.

Years ago, a friend of mine told me about an experience he had with an IBM Executive that proved to him that business deals were like a marriage. Both parties must bring something desirable to the table.

The Pay-to-Go in conjunction with the Resident Visa Program do exactly that.

At the end of the day, the United States would have no more resident illegal aliens. Instead, the former illegal aliens would either have gained a Resident Visa and would be legal, and be under the terms of their visa or they would be in their home countries cashing their massive stipend checks, while preparing to knock them dead as newly funded entrepreneurs in their home country.

Chapter 4 A Pro-American Comprehensive Immigration Program

Are words *comprehensive* and *American* incompatible?

We have already described the proposed Resident Visa Program and the Pay-to-Go program in simple terms. The Gang of Eight Senators, the term comprehensive was made a synonym of amnesty and as such it did not belong in the same sentence as American. Pay-to-Go and the Resident Visa are all-American notions that reflect the good-will of the American people in a genuinely comprehensive way. Thse programs together have wall that is needed to solve the problem of shadows and sanctuaries forever.

Can this possibly be enough to prompt Congress and the President to finally create a *pro-American, comprehensive* immigration plan. Those normal and reasonable people who read the plan will know immediately that it will work and work well.

Overall, its acceptance depends on what's in it for Americans and what is in it for Illegal Foreign National Interlopers? Let's examine the benefits for interlopers first. Yes, a pro-American plan can have lots of great benefits for illegal foreign nationals.

Both programs together provide many benefits for those currently living in the shadows. For those wanting to stay in America now have a way to gain freedom to roam and a sense of belonging and an opportunity to succeed in America.

Think about why an illegal alien residing in America in the shadows should like the Resident Visa Program? While you are thinking, consider the seventeen points beginning on the next page:

1. No more living in the shadows of America.
2. Opportunity to go home travel-free if desired with a big stipend paid by Americans.
3. US will budget $15 Billion to help make cities in home countries safe for returning immigrants
4. US will separately create 15 safe areas. They may be large settlements or perhaps small cities. Ten of these would probably be best to be built in Mexico.
5. Resident Visa Holder (RVH) can get in line (back of line) in home country for citizenship without leaving US.
6. With renewals, the opportunity to live in America a lifetime.
7. Can obtain a driver's license, insurance, etc.
8. Can keep any job that is already held.
9. Can apply for any job available in America.
10. Can live wherever they want in America.
11. Can get same *paid by patient medical insurance* as Americans.
12. Can get installment loans from US Government on an exception basis to help with medical and educational expenses. Must be paid back.
13. After ten years but no more, living with a Resident Visa, can still opt for Pay-to-Go.
14. Green Card Pay-to Go stipend of $30,000 per permanent resident.
15. Anchor person Pay-to-Go huge stipends of $50,000 per birthright citizen.
16. Green Card Resident Visa stipend of $30,000 per permanent resident for transition from permanent residency to Resident Visa.
17. Anchor citizen Resident Visa stipend of $50,000 per birthright citizen) for transition from citizen to Resident Visa.

As you can see, we included some of the benefits of the Pay-to-Go program in the list above.

Many of the advantages for current interlopers are listed in the seventeen points above. The Pay-to-Go program provides a stipend that is more generous than any other country in the world. The Resident Visa Program immediately gets interlopers out of the shadows and provides a stipend for green card holders and anchor citizens who transition from their current program to the Resident Visa Program with the option after ten years of using Pay-to-Go.

If you want to stay in America, the Resident Visa is the best plan for illegal interlopers. If you want to stay in America and receive a generous stipend, the Resident Visa transition can also be used by Green Card Holders as well as Anchor Citizens.

Knowing this is so beneficial to interlopers, why should an American find it acceptable? The answer is simple. Americans are smart and upon analysis they can see that both plans if implemented by Congress and/or the President will save a ton of dollars for all American taxpayers. Moreover, nobody really likes the shadows or the sanctuaries.

Many Americans do not trust the government, period. So, why would Americans think this is a good deal if the illegal foreign national does not choose to exit America with a stipend? Then what?

If an illegal foreign national chooses not to accept this US government act of kindness, and does not go home, and does not sign up for The Resident Visa Program, the only option left is to stay in the shadows and/or sanctuaries. This will result in the interloper being asked to leave the country at their own expense.

By the enactment of this new visa and this new "Pay-to-Go" return home" plan, the idea of residing in America in an illegal alien status is being eliminated. The lack of a decision by an illegal interloper to choose one or the other will unfortunately provoke immigration authorities to deport them.

Why should an American citizen like these two plans?

1. The days of the free lunch are over.
2. Both programs are cost free to Americans
3. Pay-to-Go stipends pay for themselves in one year
4. Illegal aliens must agree to terms of Resident Visa-- all benefits eliminated after 1st year.
5. Once an illegal alien returns home, cannot come back; no cost to Americans after year 1.

6. No more birthright citizenship for illegals, permanent residents, and Resident Visa Holders. Children born in America in future may apply for a Resident Visa.
7. No cash, medical services, education, welfare, or other benefits permitted for those with a Resident Visa.
8. No citizen-only privileges permitted
9. Resident Visa Holders have no right to vote in any election
10. New jobs must go to American citizens first—all things being equal.
11. Fees, fines on employers will help pay for Resident Visa program kickoff. Will generate approximately $400 Billion.
12. When program in high gear, US will save from 500 Billion dollars to One Trillion dollars per year on avoided interloper expenses.
13. Resident Visa holder must be employed.
14. Resident Visa holder must have health insurance.
15. Resident Visa holder must pass English test in two years
16. Resident Visa holder must take oath of allegiance to be approved for 1st renewal
17. No more green cards for family reunification-instead use Resident Visa.
18. All green card permanent residence visas are eliminated when expired. No new green cards. Use Resident Visa.
19. Next 10-yr green card renewal becomes a Resident Visa
20. No path to citizenship without going home to get in line (begin a process like all others from that country)
21. Citizenship line -- jumping the line is not permitted.
22. No more "need" for Sanctuary Cities
23. No more need for DACA Dreamers
24. Major cost savings for America

The end of Sanctuary Cities

Victor David Hanson writes: "Sanctuary cities protect illegal aliens from federal immigration agencies in a way that is not true of American citizens who arrive at airports and must go through customs, with no exemption from federal agents examining their passports and personal histories. If crimes or infractions are found, there is no safe space at an airport exempt from federal enforcement."

The new migrant programs that I am recommending either pay illegal interlopers to go or provides a Resident Visa that offers many benefits to both interlopers and American citizens. For example, it saves over $500,000,000 000 per year after year one of its implementation. With no more illegal aliens in the country, a major advantage is that the divisive notion of Sanctuary Cities and the term Sanctuary Cities can be removed from the US vocabulary. There will be no need for them with residents all being legal.

Anchor babies qualify

The Pay-to-Go Program is also available to those who became citizens through the anchor baby loophole of the 14th amendment. When an Anchor child with parent chooses to join the Pay-to-Go Program, each anchor citizen child will receive a $50,000 stipend and each of his or her interloper parents will receive their own $20,000 for a total of $70,000 for a two-person family and $90,000 for a three-person family with one child. A family of four children with a mom or dad would receive $240,000. With mom and dad, the sum would be $240,000. This is very affordable for US citizens considering the lifetime cost of one anchor baby can be as much as $2 million or more.

DACA "children" also qualify

The SRRV program solves the problem for DACA children also. DACA children qualify for the full $20,000 stipend in the Pay-to-Go Program. Those in the DACA program also qualify for the Resident Visa Program if they want to stay in the US. As an additional DACA concession for the "Children" who opt for the Resident Visa, there will be no charge for the visa for the first five renewal years. DACA "children" will be vetted when they apply for a resident passport. Gang members, of course, will be deported without benefits.

Green card holders also qualify

Green card holders, about 15,000,000 are legal permanent residents (LPR). Some are awaiting their time so they can be citizens. Others have chosen to stay legal in America without being citizens. Many are on welfare costing the US $30,000 each. Resident Green Card holders can receive a $30,000 stipend and use the Pay-to-Go option to return home, or they can receive a $30,000 stipend to downgrade their status from LPR to Resident Visa. Since Resident Visa holders do not receive welfare, this would save as much as several hundred billion dollars if all those in LPR status switched to Resident Visas or returned home.

Green card program can be eliminated

Because many in the LPR program collect welfare as an entitlement, I would recommend that the US eliminate green cards completely. All those who qualify to be citizens can be granted a Resident Visa and all other things for them would be the same. However, they would not be able to collect welfare with a Temporary visitors' visas. The US would save $Billions.

The evidence is on the table.

Nobody in their right mind wants life to continue with a shadow population who in many ways have been victimized similar to how slaves were victimized many years ago. The Pay-to-Go and the Resident Visa are programs that provide a way out of the mess for both interlopers and regular Americans.

Greedy fat cat business persons and politicians at the highest levels created this mess for both factions. Consequently, the plan includes substantial fees and fines for those businesses who hired illegal interlopers instead of Americans. Being greedy will collectively cost the fat cats over $400 Billion in total and perhaps more.

Companies made a ton of money off the backs of Americans with lower wages while poor interlopers were living in squalor earning sub-minimum wages. American industry as represented by the Chamber of Commerce should show some remorse and voluntarily chip in to help solve this problem and back the Pay-to-Go and the Residence Visa Programs as winner ideas for all decent Americans and the long-suffering communities whose only solace is the shadows of America.

Quick Comparison with the Gang of Eight

In 2013, you may recall that eight US Senators known as the Gang of Eight got a bill passed in the Senate that sold Americans down the river and would have given a ton of benefits to illegal aliens at taxpayer cost. The Pay-to-Go and the Resident Visa Programs are both pro-American and they save taxpayers substantial dollars. It is nothing like the John McCain / Marco Rubio Gof8 sellout. The following quick comparison chart is shown to help us better understand the new Resident Visa recommendation by comparing it in the chart below with the Gang of Eight Program which was passed by the US Senate.

2013 Gang of Eight v Resident Visa

	G of 8	Resident Visa, PTG
Border secure	No	More technology
Jobs	Favors Interlopers	Favors Americans
Amnesty	Yes	No
Path to citizenship	Yes	No (almost same as today)
Permanent residents	Yes	Never, renewable visa
Voting	Yes	No, Never
Welfare benefits	Yes	No, Never
Freebies	Yes	No, Never
Anchor babies	Yes	No, stipends to return / change
Employer fees/fines	No	Yes -if one illegal employee
Reunification	33M in 10yrs	Not for Resident Visa Holders
Coerced-deportation	None	As needed for violations
Return to home country	No	Yes, with stipend
Must have healthcare	No	Yes
Must be employed	No	Yes
Must speak English in 2 yrs?	No	Yes
Oath of allegiance	No	Yes, after 1 year
Cost/debt accountability	No	Yes
Taxpayer Costs	$ 6Trillion	Zero
Payback plan	No	Yes
Accountability Database	No	Yes
Interloper fine	Yes	Yes
Employer fine	No	Yes (helps finance program)
Back taxes	No	Yes (vetting interviews)

Chapter 5 Why Does the United States Have Immigration Laws

Are 60 million unwanted uninvited guests in America a problem?

In a simple word, "Yes." That is why this book explores a very clever solution that has never been tried before to the problem of having 60 million illegal foreign nationals living within the United States of America. Why is having 60 million illegal interlopers residing in the United States a problem in the first place?

Pardon my saying but it is self-evident. It is like every family of 4 in the country, getting a permanent house guest, who must be fed and watered and who must get pocket money from the family. No matter how many times asked, the "unwanted house guest" will not leave the premises.

Twenty years ago, this question of *why have immigration laws*, would have been mostly irrelevant. But, with 60 million extra people in the country, even people who never notice anything ever have been awakened by the dramatic negative effect on their lives.

Immigration Laws are not new. What is new is that government on its own decided to not conform to the people's wishes and until President Trump, they had chosen not to execute long-standing immigration laws.

Since 1790, the US has had immigration laws. In the past twenty years, our lawmakers and some presidents have not paid much attention to our laws and in many cases directly worked against the Constitution. They have intentionally violated the laws that have been duly passed by Congress and signed by the President. Can the Congress and the President violate the Constitution with impunity?

During President Obama's two terms, they ignored the Constitution, so I guess they can for they did. But it will catch up with them. America is in a quiet rebellion and greedy politicians will be the first to go.

I do not think that we are OK with unlimited illegal immigration that is bankrupting our nation and so, the only recourse for normal Americans is to replace these lawmakers. If we take no action to replace lawmakers, in essence we would be eliminating all the immigration laws and therefore letting everybody in who can afford a ticket to get here. It sure seems like that has been the government's policy as of late. No immigration plan would be necessary if we declared everybody citizens and opened up our borders 100%. So, why don't we?

In one simple answer we do not open up the border floodgates because we would be overwhelmed in one year. There are estimates that of the seven billion world population, half would migrate to the US if they could. The US currently has a population of over 325,000,000. How well would we be able to sustain our country with 1000 times that number – 325,000,000,000 which is less than half of the citizens of the world? Some estimate that within 50 years, all 325 billion who want to come, would be here. Then, what?

Maybe immigration laws do have value when we take the argument to the level that some think is ad absurdum.

When the Gang of Eight Senators passed their bill in 2013, they had wrestled with a number of contingencies and had decided that a blanket amnesty would do it. They knew those who would benefit would have been living in the US illegally for years. The citizens of the US in this case were smarter than the US Senate, and pressured the House to reject the Senate Bill. The people did not want amnesty. It stands to reason our immigration laws are there as guidelines to enforce our immigration policy. So, at some level we must have an immigration policy, right?

We've all seen politicians talk about immigration like as if citizens do not count. They like to talk about kids whose parents came here illegally and illegal immigrants who've "played by the rules" while working in the U.S. their whole lives. Rarely do they ever say that they made the laws to keep immigration sane and keep illegals out. They never say that to keep US wages up and to keep American citizens employed, they need to address the problem. e

Have you ever heard a politician tell the public just what exactly our immigration policy is supposed to accomplish? Should we not have heard something from elected officials, especially the Congress, articulating the specific goals that we are trying to achieve through our immigration policy and laws? Instead Congress haggles over retroactively granting permanent residence to those who are currently living here illegally. However, more and more of those in Congress who make such pronouncements are being replaced. The citizens are listening.

The only policy that seems to be de facto executed today appears to be that the number of immigrants the U.S. permits each year is to be defined by how many foreign nationals decide to ignore immigration laws, come on down, and choose to reside in the US. How about when a politician says that any immigration reform must include a path to citizenship for all illegals who are currently living in America. That grates on Americans.

Have you ever heard some of our finest such as Nancy Pelosi and Chuck Schumer mime parrot those lines? What they are saying is that the illegal foreign nationals themselves are the ones with the authority to determine how many people are permitted to enter the U.S. Can that be? Are our politicians that stupid, or do they think Americans are that stupid?

As we discussed in the beginning of this chapter, if we are realistic about the consequences of drastically changing our immigration policies we know what we get. For example, as noted, if we open our borders and we say that everyone on the planet who wants to live in America is now permitted with no delay or regulation or red tape, we know the US population would double, maybe triple, or quadruple, very quickly. That would probably not be such a good thing.

Most Americans believe that the U.S. should welcome good people who want a better life and who bring something positive to America but we should limit the numbers so that Americans do not suffer in any way because of such a policy. We should not permit anybody who would be a burden and we should not pay welfare for any immigrants. If you can't make it on your own, stay home. Please do not come to America. When have you heard a politician say that?

America, not illegal foreign nationals must determine what is right for America and we must manage the flow of immigrants to ensure they can be properly assimilated into American culture. We should reject those at the front door who want to change our culture and our way of life by imposing their own.

Right now, it seems that in addition to would-be perpetrators determining our immigrant policy numbers, they also determine who can come. Americans should set this goal, not foreigners. Once we set the goal, we need to determine what capabilities and values we want in an immigrant. It is our country.

Today the answer is that only those who live close-by America and who can hop the border can get in with no problem and we permit them to live in the shadows with our full knowledge. In this routine we do not even make them pass through customs to physically enter the U.S.

Don't you think that geographical proximity is a very poor qualifier for selecting who is permitted to enter the U.S. and be granted permanent resident status. We do not even check anymore for communicable diseases because people sneak in past the authorities and we simply have been letting them. Think about it!

As it stands now, 90% or better of the people being considered for any proposed legalization or path to citizenship will have come from Latin America even though Latin America has just 10% of the world's population. Is this fair? Should our immigration policy discriminate against people from Africa, Asia, Europe, and the Middle East? Why should any immigration reform we may choose to cobble together reward those whose claim to fame is that they do not have to board an airplane or boat to reach the U.S.?

If immigration reform is the elephant in the room Congress must remember that the only way to eat an elephant is one bite at a time. Let's talk about how to enforce the immigration laws that are already on the books before we create a new set of books. Then let's discuss how many people we wish to enter and reside in our country each year. How many do we want in the country? Then let's talk about the qualifications and characteristics we can use to define which people are allowed to fill that annual quota.

America is a great country but its immigration practices are being created by buffoons or as noted, by the very people we are trying to keep out of the country. I challenge the Congress to offer an honest explanation of why we have immigration laws, when they are so content to break them?

What are our laws intended to accomplish, and how must they be enforced. And, regarding the biggest ruse of all, comprehensive immigration reform; Americans need to start looking at the current use of the term *comprehensive immigration reform* as what it is –pure baloney created by baloney throwers.

!

Chapter 6 The Financial Impact of Illegal Immigration

We want America to stay America!

The Pay-to-Go program offers a unique approach to addressing the problem of having 60 million and perhaps even more illegal aliens residing in the US today. This number is overwhelming and it affects the financial stability of the country as much as it affects a number of social concerns as a group of foreigners are changing American culture either intentionally or by happenchance and perhaps both.

The new breed of resident—call them an uninvited- guest or interloper—as that is what they are, cares more about where they came from rather than the new country in which they now reside. They could care less about blending in and melting than they do about getting their fair share from America.

Americans are beginning to readily identify the culture war as it is unfolding before our eyes. With 60 million new residents, all illegal and mostly of Latino heritage, the face of America is changing as is its culture. This new war helped to set the table for the Republican presidential nomination and it certainly helped shape the mood of the country for the general elections of 2016 as Donald Trump became our 45th President.

For years, elite establishment conservatives known as the *Swamp* by real conservatives, nationalists, and populists, ignored grassroots opposition to mass immigration. Those opposed to the Swamp saw Donald Trump as the only way to gain a victory for the cause of America-first. Republicans had forgotten about their own party base.

GOP primary voters were in revolt over immigration, and they spurned elected Republicans that they no longer could trust. Donald Trump emerged as the last man standing in a field of seventeen of the top rung candidates in the Republican Party. He then defeated liberal progressive Hillary Clinton for the presidency.

Regardless of where you stand on immigration, there is no doubt that the massive post-1965 immigration wave has transformed American society. For example, about 13 percent of the U.S. population is foreign-born. This is up from 4.7 percent in 1970. And this share is set to increase substantially in the years to come. If anything, this number understates the impact of immigration on American society.

Had the post-1965 immigration wave never come, the U.S. population would today be 252 million rather than 325 million. Along the way to today, the liberals decided that the formula for who comes in legally to America to be a candidate for citizenship had to change from European to what seems to be anything but European, plus a few Irish bartenders. For immigration, countries with predominately white residents have all-but been excluded for US green cards.

Over the next 50 years, the demography experts at the Pew Research Center have calculated that new immigrants and their descendants will account for 88 percent of all population growth. My opinion is that we do not need them all. It's time to thin out the foreign-born population. That is why I created the Pay-to-Go program recommendation featured in this book. I'd like America to stay American. Anybody not willing to melt in the melting pot should stay right where they are. Please do not come on down.

Part of the reason is that the birthrate among native-born Americans has fallen to unprecedented low levels, so immigration is a much bigger part of our demographic picture than it would be had the birthrates of the post-war decades persisted into the present. This confluence of falling birthrates and surging immigration explains why the cultural character of America is changing so rapidly—too rapidly.

Perhaps if Americans were making good money like when wages were proper, before the onslaught of illegal foreign nationals, Americans would be better able to afford big families again. Just saying!

This book has a lot of great facts in it plus the opportunity to gain some different perspectives. On the financial side, there are many areas in which illegal interlopers are costing taxpayers excessive amounts of money. Look at our national debt and the budget deficits and illegal immigration as well as legal immigration and you see the effect. And the cause. Coincidentally as the debt went up, so did the influx of illegal aliens now at 60 million and growing. How much more can we take? Not much!

As you will learn, the preponderance of illegal aliens, almost half of legal aliens, and almost all birthright citizens collect some form of welfare mostly by using fake IDs with somebody else's social security number. Some are clever enough to work and collect unemployment using other-people's ID's.

Not having lots of money does not stop anybody from having large families and many of the new arrivals are immediately placed on welfare on the US taxpayer's dime. The larger the family, as we know, the greater the benefits. ID theft for anybody needing a buck for their families is not given a second thought.

There are lots of cultural and social areas, which we will be discussing in a number of chapters after this, in which the major influx of illegal foreign nationals has had a major impact on American life. In these areas, illegal foreign nationals make heavy use of the welfare system.

Overall, the costs to America for illegal interlopers in all of the areas of service in which they participate, is between $500 Billion and $1 Trillion dollars. Think about the fact that there are more welfare programs available than you or I can memorize.

The US welfare system consists of 80+ low-income programs providing cash, food, housing, medical care, and social services to poor and lower income Americans. Illegal interlopers know how to use the system for their benefit. Bleeding heart Democrat progressives have provided another huge bonanza for illegal aliens who earn just a few dollars A three-child family gets a tax-credit check from the government for $6300 each year on top of all of their welfare payments. The payment is a gift that comes out of the income tax system and does not count as welfare.

The Financial Impact of 60 million illegal interlopers

This is the short story

The best estimate you can find of US costs for illegal aliens on welfare is $30,000 for each illegal interloper each and every year. The Pay-to-Go program offers major league level stipends to three categories of foreign nationals. The categories are immediately below followed by the one-time recommended stipend amounts in addition to a free one-way return ticket home and some pocket money follows on the next page:

At 30,000 cost per year, the categories & suggested stipend amount is as follows:

	Recommended Stipend
Normal illegal foreign nationals	$20,000
Legal foreign nationals on welfare	$30,000
Birthright Citizens (Anchor Babies)	$50,000

At 30,000 cost per year, the one year cost and 1 year savings would be as follows:

	Cost	Savings (Cost - stipend)
Illegal foreign nationals	$30,000	$30,000-20,000 = 10,000
Legal foreign nationals	$30,000	$30,000-30,000 = 0
Birthright Citizens (Anchor Babies)	$30,000	$30,000-50,000 = -20,000

At 30,000 cost per year, the five year cost and 5 year savings would be as follows:

	Cost	Savings (Cost - stipend)
Illegal foreign nationals	$150,000	$130,000
Legal foreign nationals	$150,000	$120,000
Birthright Citizens (Anchor Babies)	$150,000	$100,000

At 30,000 cost per year, the twenty-year cost and 20 year savings would be as follows:

	Cost	Savings (Cost - stipend)
Illegal foreign nationals	$600,000	$580,000
Legal foreign nationals	$600,000	$570,000
Birthright Citizens (Anchor Babies)	$600,000	$550,000

At 30,000 cost per year, the lifetime cost (60 years) and lifetime savings would be as follows:

	Cost	Savings (Cost - stipend)
Illegal foreign nationals	$1.8 million	1.78 million
Legal foreign nationals	$1.8 million	1.77 million
Birthright Citizens (Anchor Babies)	$1.8 million	1.75 million

Of course, we all know that with inflation, the dollar numbers will be larger but the figures in the three charts above are representatives of the savings for each illegal interloper who takes the Pay-to-Go stipend and returns home. The bottom line is that once we pay the stipends for these categories of stipend candidates, the net gain to America is between 1.75 and 1.8 million dollars per candidate over their lifetimes.

Let's just suppose that 2 million take the offer. The twenty-year savings would be as follows:

At 30,000 cost savings after year 1 / 2, the twenty-year savings for 2 million Pay-to-Go's is as follows:

	Savings
Illegal foreign nationals	$1,160,000,000,000
Legal foreign nationals	$1,140,000,000,000
Birthright Citizens (Anchor Babies)	$1,100,999,050,000

At 30,000 cost savings after year 1 / 2, the twenty-year savings for 10 million Pay-to-Go's is as follows:

	Savings
Illegal foreign nationals	$5,800,000,080,000
Legal foreign nationals	$5,700,000,070,000
Birthright Citizens (Anchor Babies)	$5,500,000,050,000

As you can see there is a lot to save in the above two charts. Multiply the savings in the last chart above to find the lifetime savings (60 years) for 10 million acceptances of the Pay-to-Go offer. The US would be looking at over $15 Trillion in savings

Think about how difficult it would be for the US to handle all of the costs associated with illegal interlopers if the Congress fails to implement a Pay-to-Go program.

The fact is that with more and more illegals showing up at our doorsteps and visa holders brazenly breaking our laws and refusing to go home and then applying and receiving welfare to boot, please think of the devastation that not acting now with the Pay-to-Go program will create for our progeny. Can America survive?

Chapter 7 The Social / Cultural Impact of Illegal Immigration

First, the short story

When the founders created our country, they called it the United States. However long before the revolution, there was the discovery of America by Christopher Columbus. Subsequently, there were several journeys by Amerigo Vespucci. Columbus' Trans-Atlantic route lay the foundation for future navigation in the region. Maps created by Columbus were used by Amerigo Vespucci (after whom the American continent takes its name).

So few people were in America after its 1492 discovery from across the seas that when credit came to Vespucci and the country was named America, there were no protesters suggesting a better name such as Columbia or Vespuccia, And, so the US got to keep its birth name, America.

The people had their encampments and they got together for common defense in the early days because there were already people in America when they had arrived. Since the original explorers thought they were headed for India when they got here, they called the native Americans *Indians*. There was no disrespect intended and none taken at least in the early days.

In the early days, the French stayed with the French and English stayed with English and the Spanish stayed with the Spanish. Life was not always OK with the original Americans as in the depictions of The First Thanksgiving.

For example, the Indian Massacre of 1622 took place in the English Colony of Virginia, in what is now the United States. It was a horrible experience. On Friday, March 22, 1622. Captain John Smith, related in his History of Virginia that braves of the Powhatan "came unarmed into our houses with deer, turkeys, fish, fruits, and other provisions to sell us". The Powhatan grabbed any tools or weapons available and killed all the English settlers they found, including men, women, and children of all ages. "

"Chief Opechancanough led a coordinated series of surprise attacks by the Powhatan Confederacy that killed 347 people, a quarter of the English population of the Virginia colony. Eventually because the common defense became very important, everybody soon became American."

Thus, over time, people from various encampments began to know each other and there was intermarrying and as the thirteen colonies came into being, the people were getting comfortable thinking they were American, rather than French or German or English or Spanish.

Just about everybody was white as that was where all of the people came from. There were no racists then at least. The slave trade, which eventually came forth from Europe had not become a big business in America yet and would not for some time.

Out of all the country cultures, a new one was emerging that was American. There are no documented issues about culture bleed or social issues with an influx of immigrants until about 1965. More and more elite rich people emerged in America—some from old-world wealth and others from new-found industries. Clever people could make a killing in America if they worked hard. It was called entrepreneurialism.

American lawmakers had created enough laws to safeguard the country from too many immigrants but by 1965, even the government was not paying attention. Political parties such as the Republicans and the Democrats had their own ideas independent of the laws as to how to deal with immigration. They chose to ignore the laws.

The Democrats enjoyed thinking about making every minority in America and those not yet here into a Democrat and they loved the fact that if they made it easy for interlopers to sneak into America undetected, eventually they could make them registered Democrats and their Party would rule America for years to come.

Republicans chose not to fight to win. Instead they did their best to please their donors, who were mostly greedy businessmen hoping to pay Americans the smallest wage possible They call that Labor Arbitrage and it was practiced first by the Robber Barons at the end of the 19th Century. It helped a lot of otherwise small businessmen become millionaires and very important people. All they had to do was pay the smallest wage possible that would cause an American to get up in the morning and go to work.

In the mid-20th century, the descendants of this group of mercenaries found that illegal interlopers, fearful of deportation would literally work for peanuts if there were just enough to feed their families. The American middle class had already emerged and many were doing quite well, even those who worked in traditionally blue-collar jobs—such as the auto industry and others and the trades. Post-war prosperity had hit America and everybody was doing well, even minority citizens in industries such as meatpacking were well into the middle class at this time.

Becoming billionaires was not enough for the new corporatists as they looked for ways to increase profits and become wealthier than their big-shot next door neighbors—acres or even miles away. They went to church, they say, but they were far from Christian, doing their best to assure that those not doing well, would do worse and those who were doing OK, would absorb a major downturn in their wages.

To the extent they could, businessmen offshored as much manufacturing as they could--taking their former American jobs with their factories to other countries. Another vehicle, which these nasty businessmen employed was the subtle threat of replacing the workforce in America with non-citizens, who were not even legal.

Once in America, this new breed of potential workers would sign up for anything that helped them; regardless of the impact that it had on the American employees who had been holding the jobs they received.

Like all successfully orchestrated changes in cultures, this was incremental. It happened a city at a time; a company at a time; and sometimes a whole county at a time. But, it did not happen all at once or it would have been shut down quickly—I think!

So, the first impact was in wages being lowered and then the next impact was jobs not even being available. The middle class was being eroded by a huge number of illegal foreign nationals whose employers seemed to have something on the politicians who were supposed to assure this could never happen to the American public.

Here we are in 2018, and it is only getting worse. Even white-collar jobs are being given to legal and illegal foreign nationals because today's businesses have figured out, just like the robber barons of old, how to make US citizens grovel to make as much as a dollar more in salary.

The purpose of this part of the book is so that we can introduce the aspects, cultural and social, as to why we must solve the problem of 60 million illegal foreign nationals living unfettered in a country that openly says *none of that, please...a*s part of its law base.

In the seven books I wrote about immigration prior to this one, I always tried to come up with a solution for the 60 million illegal residents in America, I always had to ask myself, "why do the people want these illegal interlopers removed." But, I knew!

- Taxation Without Representation
- Americans Need Not Apply
- No Amnesty; No Way!
- The Lifetime Guest Plan
- The US Immigration Fix
- 60 million illegal aliens in America
- Pay-to-Go

In an earlier chapter of this book, I outlined financial reasons why Americans do not want to be stuck with supporting the needs of so many interlopers. If illegal interlopers simply behaved as angels and saints as their benefactors suggest that they already do, they would not at all be noticeable. However, they do not blend well with Americans and I am inclined to believe it is intentional. They do not behave as angels and saints. They like keeping their cultures and are not as interested as being Americans as earlier immigrants.

What are some of the points in which illegal foreign nationals do not blend?

- Their illegal perpetration into America creates urban sprawl
- Illegal interlopers unwittingly spread communicable diseases
- Illegal aliens work against sustaining the environment
- Illegal aliens affect the quality of K-12 US education
- Illegal aliens have a major impact on jobs that can be held by millennials and seasoned employees
- Negative impact on majority Americans
- Negative impact on minority Americans
- Crime, shadow living, and sanctuaries
- Negative impact on health care
- High incarceration rate

After this chapter, we will present several additional chapters on the cultural and social impact of 60 million illegal interlopers living in the shadows of America. We will begin with crime

Chapter 8 Crime, Shadows, Sanctuary Cities & Gangs

Illegal aliens begin as criminals

In January 2017 shortly after his inauguration, President Donald J. Trump signed an executive order that directed the Secretary of Homeland Security to publish a weekly list of "criminal actions committed by aliens." It is no secret that illegal aliens commit their first crime by breaking in or overstaying their visas and then ID theft is the next one they find necessary. Trump noted in his order that:

"Many aliens who illegally enter the United States and those who overstay or otherwise violate the terms of their visas present a significant threat to national security and public safety," the order states. "This is particularly so for aliens who engage in criminal conduct in the United States."

The order also calls for the establishment of an Office for Victims of Crimes Committed by Removable Aliens, to, among other things, study "the effects of the victimization by criminal aliens present in the United States."

The office is called VOICE—Victims of Immigration Crime Engagement. Trump explained its purpose: The purpose is to provide a voice to those who have been ignored by our media, and silenced by special interests."

Apologists for those aliens who commit crimes cite in their statistics that of all the illegal immigrants in America (11 million as their basis) far less than one million have criminal records. Assuming the criminal group will be dealt with by President Trump's deportation efforts, that leaves 10 million who will not be subject to criminal expedited processing though identity theft would surely get an American citizen locked up for a long period.

Here is the law for American citizens:

Aggravated identity theft is punishable by a mandatory minimum sentence of imprisonment for two years or by imprisonment for five years if it relates to a terrorism offense. At least thus far, the government has rarely prosecuted the five-year terrorism form of the offense. The two-year offense occurs when an individual knowingly possesses, uses, or transfers the means of identification of another person, without lawful authority to do so, during and in relation to one of more than 60 predicate federal felony offenses (18 U.S.C. 1028A).

Illegal aliens commit more crime than natives. There is a 2001 study that takes country of origin and geographic concentration factors into account found that Mexican immigrants "commit between 3.5 and 5 times as many crimes as the average native.

Today's press wants us all to believe that illegal aliens behave like angels and saints. When they discuss the crimes of immigrants, they use the legal immigrant stats because these folks must behave or they lose their green cards and are deported. However, they fail to discuss the fact that illegal aliens commit many more crimes than American citizens because it does not fit their liberal progressive agenda.

Since there is no golden database that can be tapped to get the actual facts, the overall picture of immigrants and crime remains confused. However, there is recent government data that indicates that there are many legitimate public safety reasons for local law enforcement to work with federal immigration authorities. In recent years there seems to be a major cover-up on facts that damage the claim that illegal aliens are angels and Americans are the bad guys. Folks, illegal aliens are not angels and they are not saints. Americans are the good guys. It is our country; not theirs.

Two government reports are out that help clarify the fact dilemma. The first report (GAO-05-337R) found that criminal aliens make up 27 percent of all federal prisoners. Yet according to a Center for Immigration Studies, non-citizens are only about nine percent of the nation's adult population. Thus, judging by the numbers in federal prisons alone, non-citizens commit federal crimes at three times the rate of citizens. That is not good news for illegal interloper apologists.

The findings in the second report (GAO-05-646R) are even more disturbing. This report got specific. It looked at the criminal histories of 55,322 aliens that "entered the country illegally and were still illegally in the country at the time of their incarceration in federal or state prison or local jail during fiscal year 2003."

Those 55,322 illegal aliens had been arrested 459,614 times, an average of 8.3 arrests per illegal alien, and had committed almost 700,000 criminal offenses, an average of roughly 12.7 offenses per illegal alien. They say once you commit a crime, the next one is easier to commit. Don't be fooled by reports that want to blame Americans first.

Ironically, due to political correctness and the agencies responsible for enforcing immigration laws being more liberal progressive than pro-American, there have been few studies done recently. Government bureaucrats do not want to make it look like 60 million illegal interlopers residing in the shadows is a problem so they don't report it.

The Kate Steinle story makes me sick inside.

Kate Steinle, (picture on right below on the next page) was a beautiful young lady who happened to be in the wrong place at the wrong time. Regardless, she should not have been gunned down by an illegal immigrant for lots of reasons. Nonetheless, on July 1, 2015, 32-year-old Kathryn Steinle was shot by an illegal alien named Juan Francisco López-Sánchez (picture on left above).

López-Sánchez fired a .40 caliber handgun on Pier 14 in the Embarcadero district in San Francisco. ... The shooting sparked controversy and political debate over San Francisco's status as a sanctuary city.

Jim Steinle, the father of Kate Steinle who was shot and killed on this pier in San Francisco called on Congress today to pass legislation that would take "undocumented felons off our streets for good."

Jim Steinle, Kate's father, watched her life ebb away as she died in his arms. Jim Steinle pulled no punches in his testimony before Congress: "The U.S. has suffered a self-inflicted wound in the murder of our daughter by the hand of a person that should have never been on the streets of this country," Steinle told Senate Judiciary panel during an oversight hearing on immigration policy.

Steinle's alleged shooter, Francisco Sanchez, had five previous convictions for re-entry after deportation, according to court records, and seven prior felony convictions.

You make the call. Would Katie Steinle be alive today if public officials had not told law enforcement to stand down in so called *sanctuary cities*, even when Americans are at risk?

Preventing the admission of criminals has long been a concern to the public and policy makers. Yet today's lawmakers do nothing. Even in the colonial period, there were laws against the arrival of criminals. Laws barring admission to the United States for those who have committed certain crimes remain in force today. A significant share of the public seems to believe that immigrants commit a disproportionate share of crime. They are correct.

High-profile and sometimes tragic crimes committed by illegal aliens have prompted state and local officials to pledge action to rid the community of criminal aliens. Yet, here we are no better prepared to protect Kate Steinle today than when she was gunned down. It is time to abandon political-correctness and adopt an America-First theme that President Trump has so often promised.

Josh Wilkerson's beaten to death by Illegal Immigrant

RICHMOND, Va. — Laura Wilkerson, a Texan whose son Josh was murdered by an illegal alien in 2010, who would have qualified for amnesty under a DREAM Act-like law, emotionally broke down and cried during her speech here at Jefferson Park in downtown Richmond on a Monday night at the first stop of the "Stop Amnesty Tour."

Laura said He was from Belize. She spoke about him to set the stage. He was:

"brought here illegally by his parents when he was about 10 years old. I'm just going to tell you the story. It's sad story. If I cry, don't let it bug you. It's part of my daily routine at this point. I hope that it makes you mad, because I think Josh deserved to live if only because he was an American citizen."
…

You won't believe how nasty and unremorseful, the 19-year perpetrator was and when he got on the stand, he was proud of what he had done to Josh.

"… We found out later that what he [Hermilio Moralez] did was he asked Josh for a ride home from school and Josh said, 'sure,'" Mrs. Wilkerson said. "I think he'd given him a ride home two or three times before. He took him actually to his parents' house. For some reason, we found out later why, what he did to Josh was he hit him in the nose, and this is what the kid tells from the stand, he hit him in the nose so hard that it would blind him so that he couldn't fight back. Then he kicked him so hard in the stomach. Josh was about this big around and he weighed about 100 pounds in the body bag. He kicked him so hard in the stomach that his liver sliced in two and his spine sliced in two. He ruptured his spleen. He took a closet rod and beat Josh over the head so hard with it that it broke in four pieces. He strangled him, then let him go. Strangled him, let him go. "

"Per the medical examiner, it was just torturous. After he murdered him, as he said, when Josh quit having bloody bubbles come out of his nose, he knew he was gone, he tied him up like an animal with about 13 ropes from his the back of his neck to the back of his hands, to the back of his feet. He covered his head with his school shirt. Then he put him in the back of my son's truck and he drove around and he took two dollars out of Josh's wallet and he stopped and bought gas. Then he took him to a field and he took his wallet and school ID out and just placed it by the body. Then he doused him with gas and set him on fire. It was just incredible. You just don't even believe something like this will happen to your family, let alone to just your kid.".

"What we saw in the beginning of the trial, in the opening, was the police going out to this itty bitty trail and there you saw, when they finally got to Josh, you finally saw him in the fetal position, barefooted, charred, bound up. The policeman said he looked like a doll. He didn't even look real. He looked so tiny. Then after that in the trial the next picture was of his face after they removed his shirt. It was horribly disfigured by the closet rod. So one of the last pictures I saw of Josh was one where his face is just — one of his eyebrows is here, and the other is very low. It's something you don't want to be reminded of."

Mrs. Wilkerson said that during the trial, Moralez "was proud on the stand."

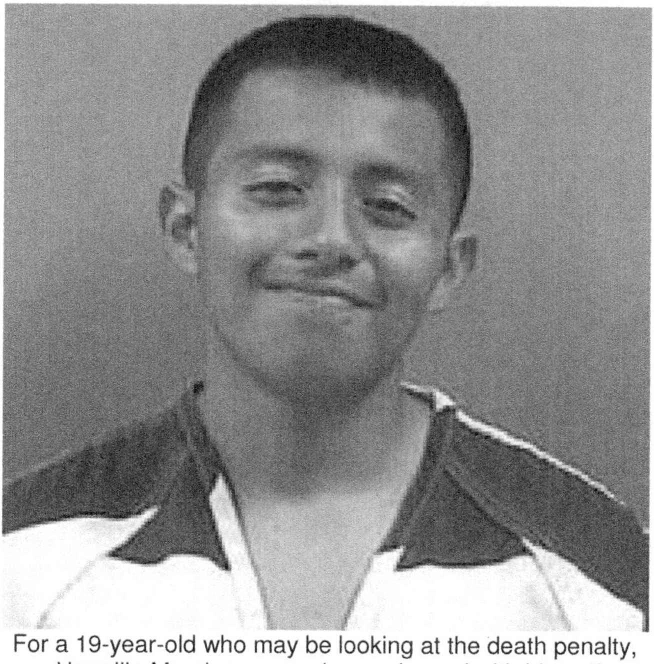

For a 19-year-old who may be looking at the death penalty, Hermilio Moralez seemed very pleased with himself

No, not all illegal immigrants behave like this but isn't one enough? Do you think sanctuary cities really help people who abide by the law?

Another very recent story to make the point

In October 2017, the Collins County Courthouse in Texas offered no solace to a woman grieving the loss of her husband and two of her children. Courtney Hacking, who lost her whole family in an auto accident with an illegal alien found no justice and she was compelled to call the two-year sentence imposed on the illegal alien responsible for the car crash that killed three innocent people, "a slap on the wrist."

"Today for me is offensive to our family," Hacking said in court. "There's no justice in what you're getting today."

The perpetrator, Margarito Quintero Rosales was sentenced to two years in prison for criminally negligent homicide. Rosales, 35. pleaded guilty to three counts of criminally negligent homicide in the deaths of Peter Hacking, 36, and the couple's children, 4-year-old Ellie Bryant and 22-month-old Grayson Hacking.

Quintero was driving a Ford van that swerved into oncoming traffic on State Highway 78 in Wylie shortly after 2 p.m. March 31, 2016, and struck Hacking's vehicle. Quintero had no driver's license.

Investigators believe that he fell asleep at the wheel. Since he already spent 537 days in jail, he'll be out in less than a year after negligently wiping out a whole family.

It wasn't the first time in court for Quintero and this sentence is being served at the same time as a two-year federal sentence imposed earlier this month. Quintero had pleaded guilty to a federal charge of re-entry of a deported alien. A Mexican citizen, the perpetrator had previously been removed from the U.S. in October 2008. Regardless of what the illegal immigration apologists suggest, this was not a victimless crime. No apology will bring back Courtney Hacking's family. make

FAIR offers the following stories on its web site FAIRUS.ORG

Tessa Tranchant killed by illegal alien

Tessa Tranchant, 16, was killed on March 30, 2007 in Virginia Beach, Virginia. Tessa and her friend, Ali Kunhardt, were sitting at a stoplight when Alfredo Ramos, an illegal alien from Mexico who was intoxicated and speeding, rear-ended their car. Ramos had a history of prior convictions, but due to Virginia Beach's sanctuary policies, he was never detained. He was charged with two counts of involuntary manslaughter and sentenced to 40 years in prison.

Sarah Root killed by illegal alien

Sarah Root, 21, from Omaha, Nebraska was killed on January 31, 2016. Her SUV was rear-ended by Eswin Mejia, an illegal alien from Honduras, who was street racing. Sarah had just graduated from Bellevue University with a 4.0 GPA the day before she passed away. Omaha is in Douglas County, Nebraska which has sanctuary policies that impede local law enforcement's ability to cooperate with ICE officers. Mejia was charged with motor vehicular homicide but posted bond to get out of jail and was released. He is still on the run.

Shayley Estes killed by illegal alien

Igor Zubko, an illegal alien from Russia, killed Shayley on July 24, 2015 in Phoenix, Arizona. Shayley obtained an order of protection against Zubko just 10 days before her murder, but he entered her home and fatally shot her. Zubko entered the U.S. legally, but overstayed his visa and remained in the U.S. illegally. He is in police custody and faces first-degree murder charges.

Drew Rosenberg killed by illegal alien

Drew Rosenberg, 25

Roberto Galo, an unlicensed driver from Honduras who entered the U.S. illegally but earned temporary protective status (TPS), killed Drew Rosenberg, a second-year law student, on November 16, 2010 in San Francisco, California. Rosenberg was riding his motorcycle when Galo ran over him three times with his car. Galo was convicted of vehicular manslaughter and sentenced to 6 months in jail. USCIS refused to deport him and he was released after serving only 43 days. Thanks to the Rosenberg family's activism, Galo was finally deported on April 4, 2013.

The number one responsibility of the federal government is to protect the citizenry. We have been betrayed by successive administrations who have allowed campaign contributions and votes to supersede that responsibility with the result being the deaths of tens of thousands of our loved ones.

The above is a note from Don Rosenberg, Drew's father

Here are some facts I got in a recent email:

Facts!

1. 43% of all FOOD Stamps are Given to Illegals
2. 95% of Warrants issued for Murder in Los Angeles are for Illegals
3. Less than 2% of Illegals are picking crops but 41% are on Welfare
4. More than 66% of ALL births in California are to Illegals on Medi-Cal
5. 60% of all HUD occupied properties in the US are Illegals
6. 39% of All California Students are Illegals
7. 75% of Los Angeles Most Wanted Criminals are Illegals
8. 50% of All Gang Members are Illegals
9. U.S. Taxpayers are Footing the Bill for ALL

Gang Problems in America

One of the major areas in which the social and cultural values of America is being affected is with the rise of gangs brought to America by the large influx of illegal foreign nationals. I will close this chapter with a transcript of the testimony given by Heather Mac Donald on Immigration and the Alien Gang Epidemic: Problems and Solutions. If you do not already know what is in her testimony, plan to be shocked at how bad it really is today in America after the close of the Obama years. Pay-to-Go and the Resident Vis plan solve 100% of the problem with illegal aliens. Here is the transcript of the testimony:

Here is some revealing testimony by Heather Mac Donald on the topic of Immigration and the Alien Gang Epidemic: Problems and Solutions. This will anger all Americans.

Heather Mac Donald

April 13, 2005

My name is Heather Mac Donald. I am a senior fellow at the Manhattan Institute for Policy Research, a think tank in New York City. I have analyzed illegal immigration for City Journal and the Los Angeles Times, among other publications. I have also written a book on policing called Are Cops Racist? I appreciate the opportunity to testify today on this important topic.

Sanctuary laws are a serious impediment to stemming gang violence and other crime. Moreover, they are a perfect symbol of this country topsy-turvy stance towards illegal immigration.

Sanctuary laws, present in such cities as Los Angeles, New York, Chicago, Austin, Houston, and San Francisco, generally forbid local police officers from inquiring into a suspect immigration status or reporting it to federal authorities. Such laws place a higher priority on protecting illegal aliens from deportation than on protecting legal immigrants and citizens from assault, rape, arson, and other crimes.

Let's say a Los Angeles police officer sees a member of Mara Salvatrucha hanging out at Hollywood and Vine. The gang member has previously been deported for aggravated assault; his mere presence back in the country following deportation is a federal felony. Under the prevailing understanding of Los Angeles sanctuary law (special order 40), if that officer merely inquires into the gangbanger's immigration status, the officer will face departmental punishment.

To get the felon off the street, the cop has to wait until he has probable cause to arrest the gangbanger for a non-immigration crime, such as murder or robbery. It is by no means certain that that officer will successfully build a non-immigrant case against the gangster, however, since witnesses to gang crime often fear deadly retaliation if they cooperate with the police. Meanwhile, the gangbanger is free to prey on law-abiding members of his community, many of them immigrants themselves.

This is an extraordinarily inefficient way to reduce crime. If an officer has grounds for arresting a criminal now, it is perverse to ask him to wait until some later date when maybe, if he is lucky, he will have an additional ground for arrest.

Sanctuary laws violate everything we have learned about policing in the 1990s. Police departments across the country discovered that utilizing every law enforcement tool in their tool chest against criminals yielded enormous gains. Getting criminals off the streets for seemingly minor crimes such as turnstile jumping or graffiti saved lives. Gang crime, which exploded 50% from 1999 to 2002, is too serious a problem to ignore this lesson.

No one knows for certain the percentage of illegals in gangs, thanks in large part to sanctuary laws themselves. But various estimates exist:

--A confidential California Department of Justice study reported in 1995 that 60 percent of the 20,000-strong 18th Street Gang in southern California is illegal; police officers say the proportion is actually much greater. The bloody gang collaborates with the Mexican Mafia, the dominant force in California prisons, on complex drug-distribution schemes, extortion, and drive-by assassinations. It commits an assault or robbery every day in L.A. County. The gang has grown dramatically over the last two decades by recruiting recently arrived youngsters, most of them illegal, from Central America and Mexico.

--Immigration and Customs Enforcement conservatively puts the number of illegals in Mara Salvatrucha as a majority; police officers, by contrast, assert that the gang is overwhelmingly illegal.

--Law enforcement officials estimate that 20% of gang members in San Diego County are illegal, according to the Union-Tribune.

-- The L.A. County Sheriff reported in 2000 that 23% of inmates in county jails were deportable, according to the New York Times.

--The leadership of the Columbia Lil Cycos gang, which uses murder and racketeering to control the drug market around Los Angeles MacArthur Park, was about 60 percent illegal in 2002. Francisco Martinez, a Mexican Mafia member and an illegal alien, controlled the gang from prison, while serving time for felonious reentry following deportation.

-- In Los Angeles, 95 percent of all outstanding warrants for homicide in the first half of 2004 (which totaled 1,200 to 1,500) targeted illegal aliens. Up to two-thirds of all fugitive felony warrants (17,000) were for illegal aliens.

--The Los Angeles Police Department arrests about 2500 criminally-convicted deportees annually, reports the Los Angeles Times.

Though the numbers of illegal gang members remain elusive, the evidence for the destructive effects of sanctuary laws is incontrovertible. In 2002, for example, four illegal Mexicans, accompanied by one legal immigrant, abducted and brutally raped a 42-year-old mother of two near some railroad tracks in Queens, New York. The New York Police Department had already arrested three of the illegal aliens numerous times for such crimes as assault, attempted robbery, criminal trespass, illegal gun possession, and drug offenses. But pursuant to New York sanctuary policy, the department had never notified the INS.

Five months ago, Carlos Barrera, an illegal Mexican in Hollywood, Ca., mugged three people, burglarized two apartments, and tried to rape a five-year-old girl. Barrera had been deported four years ago after serving time for robbery, drugs, and burglary. Since his reentry following deportation, he had been stopped twice for traffic violations. But thanks to special order 40, the police had never mentioned him to the immigration authorities, reports the New York Times.

In September, 2003, the Miami police arrested a Honduran visa violator for seven vicious rapes. The previous year, Miami cops had had the suspect in custody for lewd and lascivious molestation. Pursuant to Miami's sanctuary law, however, the police had never checked his immigration status. Had they done so, they would have discovered his deportable status, and could have forestalled the rapes.

Cousins Aneceto and Jaime Reyes committed murder and a car-jacking, respectively, after returning to Los Angeles from Mexico following deportation. The Los Angeles police had encountered them before these most recent crimes, but had to wait for them to commit murder and a car-jacking before they could lay a finger on them for their immigration offenses, according to the New York Times.

The Los Angeles Police Department began revisiting special order 40 last month. Its proposed revision merely underlines how perverse our attitudes towards illegal alien criminals remain.

Los Angeles' top brass propose to allow a Los Angeles officer who suspects that a criminal has previously been deported to contact his supervisor about the reentry felony. That supervisor would then contact ICE. ICE officials would next go before a federal judge to get an arrest warrant for the immigration felony. Then, with warrant in hand, the Los Angeles cop may finally arrest the felonious gangbanger if he can still find him.

This burdensome procedure is preposterous. To arrest an American citizen for a crime, arrest warrants are rarely required; about 95% of arrests of citizens are warrantless. But in L.A., under the new rules, illegal criminals will have due process rights that citizens can only dream of: not just judicial review before they can be taken off the streets, but federal judicial review the gold standard of all constitutional protections. Maybe home-grown criminals should renounce their citizenship and reenter the country illegally. It would be a constitutional windfall for them.

Other jurisdictions that are reconsidering their sanctuary laws are also proceeding with unnecessary timidity. The Orange County, Ca., sheriff plans to train a few deputies to use immigration laws only for special enforcement actions against sexual predators or gangs, reports the Los Angeles Times. The Miami Police Department will join with ICE only on high-level gang cases.

These minor tinkerings--all put unwise limitations on a vital law enforcement power. Local immigration enforcement power should not be limited to the felony of reentry following deportation. Nor should only a small subset of officers be authorized to use it. There are many illegal alien criminals who have not yet reentered following deportation, but who are just as dangerous to their communities. Every officer should have the power to enforce any immigration violation against a criminal suspect, not just immigration felonies.

Nothing demonstrates the necessity of this power better than ICE March enforcement action against Mara Salvatrucha. Following the March round-up, ICE proudly displayed three of its trophy cases: the founding member of MS-13 in Hollywood, Ca., who had already been convicted for robbery and possession of a dangerous weapon; the leader of MS-13 in Long Branch, NJ, who had a prior criminal history of aggravated arson, weapons possession, grand larceny, and criminal possession of stolen property; and the founder of Port Washington, NY, MS gang, who had a prior drug conviction.

ICE got all three of these leading gang bangers off the streets through what it calls administrative immigration violations, not felony immigration violations. Local officers in Hollywood, Long Branch, and Port Washington, as elsewhere, should have the power to use any type of immigration violation as well to get a thug (who may also prove to be a terrorist) off the street.

Immigration enforcement against criminals should also not wait upon a major federal-local gang initiative. The majority of opportunities to get criminals off the streets come from enforcing misdemeanors and quality of life offenses. While the police are waiting to make a major federal case against an illegal criminal, they are far more likely to have picked him up for a petty theft or an open-container offense. Officers should be empowered at every arrest or lawful stop to check someone immigration status. If a suspect is committing an immigration offense, the officer should be empowered to arrest him immediately for that offense.

Jails and prisons should routinely check the immigration status of their prisoners. Such an initiative should not be dependent on the presence of an ICE officer stationed in a prison; there are simply not enough federal agents available to cover the relevant facilities. Moreover, ICE agents do not routinely visit local jails where misdemeanor offenders are held, yet those offenders may be as dangerous to the community as someone against whom a felony case has been made. Someone convicted of stealing a jacket today may be shooting a rival tomorrow. And many misdemeanor convicts in jails have been allowed to plead down from more serious felonies.

The standard argument for sanctuary laws is that they encourage illegal aliens to work with the police or seek government services. This argument is based on myth, not evidence. No illegal alien advocate has ever provided a shred of evidence that sanctuary laws actually accomplish their alleged ends. Nor has anyone shown that illegal aliens are even aware of sanctuary laws. The evidence for the destructive effects of sanctuary laws is clear, however.

The idea that sanctuary laws are pro-immigrant is perhaps the greatest myth of all. Keeping illegal criminals in the community subjects all immigrants to the thrall of crime and impedes economic growth in immigrant communities.

Obviously, the final prerequisite for ridding immigrant communities of illegal thugs is enough ICE detention space and deportation resources. But providing police officers with every lawful tool to fight crime is a crucial first step to protecting immigrant lives and should be the unanimous recommendation of the Subcommittee.

End of Heather Mac Donald Testimony

Chapter 9 More on Non-Financial Impact of Illegal Immigration

Somebody turned on the faucet

Legal and illegal immigration into the United States has fluctuated throughout the 20th and the 21st centuries because of varying economic conditions in the sending countries. The changes made by the Immigration Reform and Control Act of 1986 was a major factor in the increasing numbers of immigrants into the US.

It was what can easily be called a dramatic increase in the number of immigrants permitted into the United States. Those not permitted by law took Bob Barker's call and simply *came on down* by illegally crossing the border or overstaying their visa. Overall, this has had a negative impact on the quality of life of many Americans today due to the colossal increase in the population and other close-to-home factors.

Worse than that, the massive illegal immigration alone has been devastating and nobody yet seems ready and willing to stop it. Successive Congresses and Presidents have decided that they want it as it is and they took no reasonable action to abate the flow of illegal immigrants into the country.

In one opportunity after another over the last decade, Congress and the President at the time declined to approve measures known to be effective to slow the flow of illegal immigrants. In fact, they clearly decided to end various kinds of enforcement that had once been effective, and they approved a series of rewards, financial and otherwise, to those who violated immigration laws.

American citizens continue to pay through the nose to support illegal aliens and many are convinced in their hearts that the illegal aliens have a much better deal than the citizens of the US today. Most blame the Congress. The eight years of President Obama made immigration control into a joke.

Unending immigration, both legal and illegal continued during the first decade of the new century. Immigration reform legislation, which often was nothing more than amnesty, was voted on multiple times. The attempts by the Congress would have provided legal permanent residence and even citizenship to the more than 10 million illegal aliens. Whenever the talk of these deals dominated the news, illegal immigration would substantially increase. Action on the southern border was so intense that apparently when talk got tough, last chance efforts to cross the border were taken at a much faster rate.

Large-scale amnesty bills failed in the Senate on multiple occasions, leading to the drafting of more focused amnesty legislation including the DREAM Act, and then DACA. The more that the people understood that the government was working against them, the more legislators got the message that if they wanted to remain in office, they had better not be so blatantly in favor of foreign nationals over citizens. And, so the DREAM Act was defeated in 2007 and it was defeated again in 2010.

The 2010 mid-term elections saw a dramatic shift in the Immigration Balance of Power in Congress, increasing chances for legislation that would reduce overall immigration numbers. Besides this, the end of the decade brought with it a stepped-up effort to discourage illegal immigration at the state level with the passage of E-Verify laws and illegal presence laws in Arizona, South Carolina, and other states. Unfortunately, at the federal level, the Congress and the President were AWOL in putting together anything meaningful that favored Americans.

President Obama was so against immigration Control he instituted lawsuits against states such as Arizona that would not permit a free flow from Mexico. Meanwhile 26 states sued the Obama Administration for overstepping its authority. It was Obama and the foreign interlopers against the citizens of the United States.

Most Citizens see little hope for the future

Though President Trump has a plan to build a wall, the Congress is fighting him on it and many think it is doubtful the Congress will do what is right for America. The immigration explosion of the last three decades has made it impossible for Baby Boomers to ever enjoy the 1970s dream of a stabilized country—even if all immigration were stopped tomorrow.

Something must happen to put Americans first. The Census Bureau states that if immigration were reduced to just replacement level, the United States population would still be growing at the end of the century because of the momentum created by the last three decades of immigration.

Why would there be much optimism when government is in the hip pockets of lobbyists and those who want to make citizens out of illegal interlopers. Americans are well aware that the middle class shrunk in 90% of 229 metropolitan areas (metros) across the nation between 2000 and 2014. The facts were verified in a recent report released by the Pew Research Center. In half of the metros, more Americans moved from the middle-income tier to the lower-income tier than from the middle-income tier to the upper-income tier. Illegal immigration is directly responsible for the job losses.

Eleven of the top 32 metros that experienced a net decline across the income tiers, are in the Piedmont region which is between Raleigh, N.C. and Atlanta, Ga. This region experienced rapid population growth fueled by high immigration levels over the same period of time. Illegal immigrants cause lower wages. It is a fact. It is also the focus of a recent Urban Sprawl Study.

Making it even worse for Americans, not one metro that falls within the Piedmont saw a net increase across the three income tiers. That's bad news for the region, but it is just another example of how high immigration levels have had a devastating effect on American workers and their wages.

In those 25 metros that suffered the biggest wage declines, their populations grew 20% faster than the U.S. population over the 15-year span. The new Americans were not recent births, they were illegal immigrants. Many of those areas also experienced the highest increases in the nation in its foreign-born population over the same period.

Taking out the fact that it is costing the taxpayers to support these interlopers, American employees are suffering because glad-handing politicos do nothing to protect American jobs and American wages.

Managing urban sprawl

Population pressures increase economic and political pressure for sprawl, defined as "unlimited and non-continuous outward expansion." Implementing smart growth strategies is necessary but insufficient to prevent sprawl development fueled mostly by immigration. From 70 to 90 percent of sprawl nationally during 2000-2010 was caused by immigration-driven population growth. Keep in mind that even internal migration is also increased in part by secondary migration away from high-immigration areas.

Congress needs to tune-in to America

Sometimes it seems that our Congress is pushing for more American suffering so their donors will be pleased and so foreigners can get a better deal from America.

It is hard to believe but Congress just does not get it. Some in Congress are pushing for even more foreign workers. Most of those pushing for increases represent the areas that are suffering the worst. The U.S. government with Congress's blessing cleared the way for thousands more foreign workers to enter the country under temporary seasonal visas. This is not expected to help the situation.

The irony of course is that in July 2017 President Donald Trump declared a "Made in America" week and pledged to stand up for U.S.

workers. Somehow the US government is not getting the message from the top. But, with Trump in charge, eventually they will.

This came just a month after Congressional actions gave the nod for more foreign national visas. Nine members of Congress boldly sent a letter to the House Appropriations Homeland Security Subcommittee pushing for a provision to the FY17 DHS spending bill that could potentially quadruple the number of H-2B visas issued. We already have too many.

Who other than greedy businessmen and Democrats hoping the new visa holders overstay, would be rooting for the H-2B visa program to allow more foreign workers to fill temporary or seasonal jobs when employers claim that they can't find an American worker to fill the job. Humph!

Of the nine letter signers, only three members represent districts that saw a net increase in incomes across the three major tiers between 2000 and 2014. The other six, including Rep. Renee Ellmers (R-N.C.), whose district lies within the Piedmont, have seen a net decrease for its middle-income residents. Congress simply does not care to address the plight of American citizens. Helping American citizens, you see, does not play well in Hollywood.

Illegal interlopers spread communicable diseases

They bring them with them. They did not ask to be sick but they are.

There has been an increase in America of communicable diseases that our country's prior leaders had helped to eradicate many years ago. I can recall walking up to Dotson Elementary School in the 1950's to get the Oral Salk Polio Vaccine. Back then, the US Congress assured the citizens were well. It was free for everybody in the country. Polio was eradicated within a few years.

How has this new problem emerged? Well, by not giving anybody a checkup at their expense before they can go on welfare is surely one way. Sanctuary Cities in which you can't even hint that somebody may not be a bona fide American is another way to increase the number of cases of communicable diseases.

The well-known Medical Doctor from Fox, Marc Siegel offered this sallow look at the problem of Americans catching diseases eliminated years ago in these simple terms: "When you let illegal immigrants into a Sanctuary City ... It increases the rate of disease" Case closed!

It takes just a hint of logic to know that communicable diseases do not stop at international borders. They are in fact, one of the most potentially dangerous—yet rarely considered—consequences of inadequate immigration controls. Despite the obvious dangers of ignoring this risk, the mainstream media, and most liberal policy makers go out of their way to avoid any discussion of the public health threats presented by unimpeded illegal immigration.

Maybe they do not care as long as they are protected deep within their gated communities. Nonetheless, in a world where long distance travel is both accessible and affordable to many people, the possibility of our next major epidemic being traceable to unvaccinated migrants is a reality that should not be ignored. Do our representatives really care about the represented?

Anybody who reads has become acquainted with the problems of basic sanitation in third-world countries. When populations are concentrated in areas lacking basic sanitation and inadequate medical care, diseases take root and spread rapidly. The reality is so severe that it makes no sense to label this caution as an expression of xenophobia, nor a trumped-up rationale to exclude migrants as "carriers of disease." The need to control infectious disease is a simple fact of human biology. The results of ignoring this fact to accomplish a political agenda can be quite deadly

Sustaining the environment

In recent years, we all know the concern of the community of people focusing on environmental issues and their concern for over-population. Ironically, because environmentalists are typically liberals with big hearts and little common sense, they have chosen to ignore the fact that illegal aliens in America contribute to the lack of sustainability of the US environment.

The irony is that their goals are conflicted since reducing immigration, a solution for overpopulation in America, is essential to what they believe would be achieving environmental sustainability in the United States. Yet, they choose not to comment on the dichotomy.

Environmentalists are universally opposed to increasing populations anywhere. Yet, it is OK with them if the populations from anywhere move to the United States. Why is this?

I know why but it shows environmentalists are also hypocrites. We all know that being against an increasing population is OK. However, being against an increasing population caused by excessive illegal immigration is politically incorrect and thus is not OK. So how do they resolve the conundrum?

Tough choice for those who do not think but not for normal Americans. The non-thinkers must say no to the environment in order to say yes to the influx of illegal immigrants. They do not want to discuss the immutable fact that effective environmental sustainability policies will ultimately fail if U.S. immigration and population continue to grow as projected.

Education

In today's world. nothing black is black and nothing white is white. The Chairman of the Data Processing Department at King's College years ago, Angelo P. Decesaris, one of my favorite professors and a great man to boot, RIP, had a favorite saying that fits in many circumstances: 'There is no black or white…It's all grey"

US Citizens must pay for the Education of the children of illegal aliens

US taxpayers pay for everything with which the Congress cannot deal so why not education? Under a 1982 U.S. Supreme Court decision, Plyler v. Doe, states and localities across the mainland and Hawaii and Alaska cannot deny illegal interlopers access to elementary or secondary education.

The Plyler v Doe case involved a 1975 Texas law that withheld education funding for children who came to the country illegally and that allowed local schools to deny enrollment to these pupils. On a 5 to 4 vote, the Supreme Court ruled that this law violated the Fourteenth Amendment and therefore was unconstitutional.

It does not matter whether the SCOTUS got it right or not. It is now the law and this new law created a huge magnet for the children from other countries to find their way into America and get a scholarship to graduate from our public schools with no funds expended. Are the judges living in the same country as the people?

Because of liberal judges aligned with the Democrat Party, schools have no choice but at their own expense to educate children whether they are legal or illegal residents of the United States. The same logic applies to emergency health care. On the principle that everyone deserves care, hospital emergency rooms are supposed to treat patients no matter their legal status or their ability to pay.

Somebody ought to write a book on the ten thousand ways the Democrat Party has harmed our country.

In the Supreme Court decision, Lau v. Nichols in 1974, the court stated that when public schools do not provide non-English speaking children the language of instruction, they are violating the students rights. I respectfully disagree. In the Plyler vs. Doe (1982) case, public schools became required to provide education to all students regardless of immigration status and are prohibited from requiring proof of status (Ramanujan, 2009). What if the communities cannot afford the burden from other countries. Unfortunately, the courts do not care about Americans.

How could these judges have seen these cases as black and white? --to offer such overreaching rulings. Why are Americans not required to send dollars all over the world to countries that do not offer the same education Americans receive in America. How is it fair that Americans can receive such a great education in America and Africans or Belgians, or Argentinians, who find themselves wanting in education, cannot insist on an American education? Judges I am afraid, when they hear an ad absurdum argument must think it is a good idea.

Why should children they have to reside illegally in the US to get benefits? Why should the Supreme Court not rule that the US should empty its treasury so nobody in the world should go hungry? Would it matter to the SCOTUS if the US treasury is broke?

Americans in various forums have offered their thoughts:

Comment # 1 If they want to come to America, then fine, but do it legally. Illegal immigrants come to our country and take advantage of us. We shouldn't have to spend our money making sure criminals and lazy immigrants get a education. We need to spend our money helping our own children.

Comment # 2 I am not an illegal, I am hurting for an education just as much as you are. I want to advance my knowledge and succeed in life just as much as you do. Ye,s you are human. But you are illegal, so why should that make you special? I was born and raised in California and I'm struggling to pay tuition, while I watch you the illegal get a free ride. What for? Why should you be placed ahead of me? THIS IS WRONG no wonder America is no longer number one we got too soft and greedy.

Comment #3 They are ILLEGAL immigrants. While I do believe everyone has the right to get an education, they do NOT have a right to get an education in America. If they want an education do it in their country where they are a LEGAL citizen. If they want an American education then fill out the proper paperwork and make it happen. All we are doing is giving more people more reason to smuggle themselves into our country illegally and work off of our system. Our country is absolutely ridiculous for allowing this to happen. Next, they will want free money from us because they can't find a job in our country because they are illegal, oh wait... They have already asked.

They absolutely should not get an education in our country unless they go through the proper channels. That is the law. Plain and simple. I love how our government sets all of these rules in place but doesn't feel the need to follow the rules themselves.

A swelling / overcrowded education system

There are many things that every parent and every taxpayer should know about immigration and the current public education crisis. Regardless of the mainstream media and the Democratic Party's attempts to keep parents and taxpayers in the dark, public school systems in America are having a tough time doing what is right. The mainstream media and the Democratic Party are winning in a disinformation war to keep the public from knowing that dumbing down all public education only helps those who cannot speak English, and last time I checked, they are typically not American citizens.

Public school districts across the United States are suffering under a massive unfunded mandate imposed by the federal government. The feds require that poor local school districts who take as little as a dime from the feds must educate millions of illegal aliens. These are a mix of the school age children of illegal aliens, refugees and legal immigrant students.

This part of the analysis as to why Americans need a real solution to 60 million illegal interlopers residing in the shadows of US cities does not focus on the financial aspects and the major ongoing costs to taxpayers for lax immigration law enforcement. We covered the financial side of the issue several chapters ago. It is not just the taxpayers who pay but it is the students and the parents of American-born children. Parents cannot figure out why their kids must have a sub-par education just because politicians want unbridled illegal immigration to continue in this country.

The people's immigration advocacy group known as *FAIR* estimates that it currently costs public schools $59.8 billion to serve this burgeoning population of illegal alien children. And, their estimate of the illegal population is 12.5 million, not the more exact number of 60 million.

There is a big struggle across the country for regular, normal people, who happen to be American citizens to put up the money to fund programs for students with limited English proficiency (LEP), sometimes referred to as *English language learners* (ELL). Nobody suggests that this does not represent a major drain on school budgets but nobody with a liberal bent seems to care and so they are not inclined to help in any way to solve the problem.

The problem is that due to political correctness, it is taboo to raise the issue even though scarce resources are redirected away from American citizens to support programs like English for Speakers of Other Languages (ESOL) and English as a Second Language (ESL). Learn English if you want to live in America!

The major influx of newcomers to the public schools helped President Barack Obama fulfill the promise he made five days before his election in 2008 to "fundamentally transform the United States." The situation with illegal foreign nationals got worse from the moment of President Obama's inauguration.

Try on these statistics and ask yourself if they represent the formula you would introduce to make education better in the US. The facts are not very supportive of the liberal approach to education and immigration, yet, one would swear that liberals do not have children and therefore do not care. They know but being liberal and pro-illegal alien is more important than being the first-line advocates for their very own children.

Almost one in every ten students enrolled in public schools is designated as LEP. How did that happen in an America in which English is the language? Who are these people who cannot speak our language?

For kindergartners, the figure for the need for remedial English is 17.4 percent. In 2013, the Department of Education determined that the United States will require 82,408 new or trained LEP teachers by 2018—if school districts can find enough qualified candidates. Despite the growing LEP population, only 10 percent of teachers are currently certified or trained in ESL. Yet, we pay them to teach foreigners because something went wrong in America, and it must be corrected for America and Americans to survive.

What factors strain public schools?

This book cannot solve it all though if the Pay-to-Go program were adopted and were successful, this problem would eventually solve itself. Let's take the short-way out and just look at the factors creating the problem in bullet form below:

- A surge of unaccompanied alien minors crossed the border from Mexico, Guatemala,Honduras and El Salvador beginning in 2014
- Large family units are entering the country illegally
- Many people overstay their visas
- Higher-than-average birthrates among families with an illegal head-of-household
- Around a million to two-million or more legal immigrants granted permanent resident status every year since 2004
- About 400,000 birthright citizens anchor babies born each year

In addition, the spread of "sanctuary" cities, counties, etc, across the country has made the problem worse. We may think it is only cities and counties but recently two states (California and Connecticut) totally refuse to cooperate with federal immigration agencies. Now, these states and cities and counties serve as magnets for illegal aliens. Many school districts intentionally operate in an active sanctuary jurisdiction, but few politicians in those areas choose to tell the people what its social cost or its fiscal cost is to them.

School districts across the nation are affected by the children of illegal aliens. Some may be illegal aliens themselves and others may be anchor citizens. The schools are beginning to complain to the Federal Government that there is no room for their students to learn because of excessive immigration and school overcrowding.

Let's look at this briefly to gain the proper perspective.

There is an overcrowding crisis in American schools and it is directly attributable to high immigration, both legal and illegal.

In a world without facts, corrupt politicians in the Democrat Party who want every illegal's vote to count and those corrupt politicians in the Republican Party who want every illegal to accept slave wages while working for one of the Republican big-shot donors, some continue to preach that it is selfish for Americans to inhibit illegal aliens from living in America.

But, they are not the facts. Corrupt politicians actually bring a world of hell upon a vulnerable population who are not ever permitted to gain independence or even a modicum of wealth in life. Instead, they must stay in the shadows paying for the crime of not coming into the US legally.

I am truly sorry for the trouble the shadows and sanctuary population are experiencing but they could have avoided it all by staying put. They are the ones who decided it was OK to take American jobs no matter what their actions did to the average wage in the US. I am pleased to represent notions that help American citizens.

Americans know that we are hurt every day by politicians luring more and more illegal aliens into our country. Nobody wins except the politicians and the big-shot greedy US businessmen who love practicing labor arbitrage for the huge profits they receive on the backs of really poor people.

The fact is that without school-age immigrants and the children of immigrants, school enrollment would not have risen at all during the past decade.

One in every five students in school systems has an immigrant parent, more often illegal than legal. One-quarter of these children were foreign-born themselves. Nobody in government seems to care about the negative impact on the American family.

Looking ahead, nobody really would like to hear the fact that if politicians do not begin to represent Americans instead of foreign nationals, immigration will account for 96 percent of the future increase in the school-age population over the next 50 years. The dollars this costs America are nothing compared to the social cost of having a major population component that really does not care about melting into the pot called America.

The bottom line on education

The bottom line on improving education by addressing class size has a pre-ordained potential for success. If immigration continues at current rates, efforts to reduce class size and ease overcrowding will be doomed to failure.

Historical Emergence

For citizens and immigrants (legal and illegal), education is the key to a successful life. After all, one of the many advantages of living in the United States is the access to a free public education paid by school taxes which are paid by parents and residents.

In most countries, there is no public education infrastructure in place, or education, public and private, is too costly for most people to afford. For that reason, many immigrants come to the United States, believing the education they receive in the United States will better their lives or the lives of their children. This is true for illegal immigrants just as it is true for legal immigrants. But Americans are not so well endowed that we can educate the entire world though it might be nice if we could.

In 1982, the U.S. Supreme Court divined a right not given by the founders. They supported the supposed right of illegal alien students to have access to US public school education at no charge to themselves or their parents. It's on us!

The SCOTUS ruled on the case of Plyler v. Doe. This ruling essentially forced states to guarantee illegal alien students free access to a K-12 grade public school education. Furthermore, it established the rights of the children of illegal interlopers as student o be the same as the rights of citizens and legal residents. Tell me in which country the SCOTUS lives?

Though the U.S. Supreme Court's decision in Plyler v. Doe was crucial in securing foreign national students' right to a free public primary and secondary education, it did not help them to attend public and private universities and colleges across the country. But the bleeding hearts, anti-American crowd may get that changed when they get a sympathetic Congress and a sympathetic presidency the next time around

Title IV of the Higher Education Act of 1965 stipulates that the government cannot give any public financial aid to illegal foreign national for the purposes of higher education. Finally, somebody got it right. But, governments at all levels have decided that Americans can pay for aliens and so they ignore the laws.

FAIR (Federation for American Immigration Reform) on Education:

- FAIR argues that immigration is overcrowding schools, which is causing the need to build new schools.
- FAIR also states that the increase of immigrants in schools has resulted in a federal Bilingual/Immigrant State Grant program to help schools with this issue. The National Association of Bilingual Education estimates that about $700 million a year is given to school districts that experience a large necessity for this program due to the levels of immigrants in their schools.
- Overall these the lack of space causes taxpayer revenue to go towards making space instead of to improving the education for U.S. and current students. Yes, with so many students looking for a desk, funds are diverted from education to make more space available due to population growth and to contribute to new programs
- FAIR indicates that other serious problems with immigrants in the education system is that there is a high immigrant drop-out rate that has caused the high school graduation rates in the United States to drop to just 70 percent, compared to the 80 percent that the US achieved 40 years ago.

- This also causes challenges to teachers in training because they are struggling with meeting with educational challenges. For example teachers have goals in improving students achievements levels.
- Another issue that FAIR identifies is that illegal immigrants are possessing bachelor degrees and post-doctoral degrees in which they will be competing with other Americans in the job market.

Chapter 10 Tell Me About Jobs & Millenials, etc.

Illegal interlopers have become the replacement players

Illegal interlopers have become the replacement players for millennials and yet something inside of millennials keeps them from seeing the truth.

They have no problem knowing that it is old farts like their parents that are keeping the country moving while, despite their degrees, they remain unemployed.

Jobs affect the well-being of more than just millennials though the millennials are supposed to become the *replacement players* for those who have been keeping America prosperous for years. If not the millennials, who so far are not doing well, perhaps America will have to wait until the following generation matures. But, then again there are others from other countries ready to fill the bill.

Let's hope for some medical breakthroughs to help the country survive with old farts running things, while a competent future generation becomes ready.

The millennial generation, sometimes referred to as Generation Y, is well on its way to becoming a "lost generation" as many politicians continue to push for policies that will make millennials less and less significant to America's success.

Politicians are pushing for amnesty and massive increases in immigration levels. This of course puts the special interests of a narrow economic and political elite above the needs of the American people, especially millennials who wake up every day wanting a life of their own but not thinking they need to do anything to achieve it.

Facing chronic unemployment and underemployment, millennials are their own worst enemies. They have been convinced by commie-pinko coffee-breath professors who never refuse to accept their salaries in ill-focused universities, that America is bad and capitalism is bad and success itself is bad.

They have rejected notions that one must work hard to gain the rewards of their efforts. They teach the mush brain generation to drink coffee and not to listen to anybody older than thirty unless of course, they are coffee-breath professors of the finest blends. The professors and now the millennials are very happy to damn those who engage positively in the US economy to help make their lives and the lives of their young families better for now and for the future.

And thus, confronted with a future that is anything but bright, many millennials feel they should be forgiven for failing to establish stable careers, while shouldering sizeable student loan debts. Those who do not graduate from college face a labor market in which there are few available jobs paying a livable wage. They don't ever seem to go back to challenge their coffee-breath liberal, anti-American professors whom they respect ad absurdum.

In studying this phenomenon, it helps to know that between 2003 and 2012, the number of unemployed 18 to 34-year old's increased 37 percent, up to 5.7 million. Why? Well, we know that robots did not take their jobs at McDonalds and in carwashes, and in low-paying entry level positions in businesses of all kinds—at least yet.

In fact, the only reason this number is not higher is that during the same period, 3.3 million 18- to 34-year-olds simply dropped out of the labor force. Willing illegal foreign nationals gladly took their jobs, and more are ready to trip the border wires to get here.

The labor participation rate for American-born teenagers continues at an historic low, down a third, since high school dropouts, who do work, struggle to make ends meet. When the Census Bureau collects stats, even they found that the average high school dropout has minimal expectations. They know that they can expect to earn just $20,241 per year in a good year.

Besides a very low average annual salary, dropouts also face a much higher unemployment rate than the national average. Dropouts can expect little in the form of rewards. It is this group, high school dropouts, who face the major competition for jobs most directly from illegal aliens. To prove the point, from 2007 to 2013, the number of unemployed native-born persons without a high school diploma increased by 18.7 percent while the number of unemployed foreign-born persons decreased by 24.8 percent.

What does this mean? Try this on…during the "recovery" following the Great Recession, employers continued to favor illegal alien labor sources despite millions of less-educated Americans who were unemployed. True, but not good for Americans and there were no Congresspersons who became advocates for Americans, despite these nasty statistics favoring the illegal sector of our population.

Illegal aliens take any job that offers any opportunity

We all know that illegal aliens come to the United States to take jobs that offer them greater opportunity. They do not care if the jobs are already held by millennials or seniors or those Americans in-between. The interlopers are often welcomed by greedy U.S. employers who are able to hire them for wages substantially lower than they would have to pay U.S. employees.

Though such employment is illegal under a law enacted in 1986, more and more employers have chosen to ignore the law and hire illegal workers in the underground "shadow" economy. Their profits grow huge the more laws they break. In the Obama Administration, these employers may have even been invited to the White House for special honors. The former President had little regard for normal working Americans.

Many employers are happy to accept fake employment documents and hire the illegal workers as if they were legal. Because there is no requirement to verify documents presented by workers, employers can easily evade true compliance.

The illegal alien employees are mostly persons who snuck into the country—nearly all Mexicans or Central Americans who enter from Mexico. There is also illegal entry across the northern border with Canada, with apprehensions by the Border Patrol of more than 6,000 aliens in 2010.

How to become an illegal alien?

The easiest way to become an illegal alien is to arrive with a legal visa and simply stay when it expires. A significant portion of the illegal alien population began as legal visa holders. At the turn of the 21st century, 'overstayers' were estimated variously at between one- third and 40 percent of the illegal alien population.

In 2007 this changed, giving the edge to the overstayers. It has continued to go up. Two-thirds of those who joined the illegal alien population in 2017 did so by entering with a valid visa and then overstaying their period of admission.

There are too many defenders of illegal aliens—ethnic advocacy groups, employer groups, and church-based groups. They don't see the damage they do as they care only for the foreign nationals and they choose not to see the American side.

Perhaps if all these "good people," advocated for better wages and working conditions for illegal interlopers, they would be helping them a lot more than messing with immigration officials. Why such social justice minded good people think they are helping interlopers when they must know they live in squalor with fifteen others in a three-bedroom shack—is a puzzlement indeed to those of us who advocate for American citizens.

The "good people" often assert that illegal aliens only take jobs unwanted by U.S. workers. This is patently false because they are working in jobs in which U.S. workers are also employed—in construction, agricultural harvesting, or as service professions.

If the hiring of illegal alien workers is prevalent in a particular sector of the economy, as has become the case in seasonal crop agriculture, the willingness of foreign workers to accept sub-minimum wages because of their illegal status acts to depress wages and working conditions for all employees in that occupation. It is not a good deal for Americans or for the illegal interlopers.

This illegal hiring makes employment in that sector less attractive to U.S. workers who sometimes have other options. Illegal aliens who take the poor-paying jobs have a difficult time making ends meet in those professions.

The result is a form of circular logic. The more that illegal aliens are able to take jobs in a sector of the economy, the less attractive the jobs in that sector become to U.S. workers, because they depress the wages. Soon after winning over labor, and knowing it, the greedy employer boldly offers nothing but sub-minimum wages to any employee and nothing close to what had been the prevailing wage.

The circular logic adds a greater appearance of validity to the lie that only illegal aliens are willing to take jobs in that sector. Only by enforcing the immigration law against the employment of illegal alien workers can this spiral to the bottom be broken and employers forced to restore wages and working conditions to levels that will attract U.S. employees and legal foreign workers.

Of course, the Pay-to-Go program and the Resident Visa Program can serve as great equalizers for Americans if Congress has the guts to implement such positive programs.

Chapter 11 How Many US Jobs Are Taken by Illegal Aliens?

Maybe there are no answers!

There are some questions that cannot be answered with 100% certainty because there is no data bank that holds the information necessary about illegal immigration. But, there should be. In most cases, data is not even collected though again, it certainly should be.

For fifteen years from 2002 to today, the number of illegal aliens in the country as estimated by many sources has been stuck at 11 million. We all know this is impossible. It is not even debatable. It is a ruse put forth by Democrats who want more voters and Republicans who want more sub-minimum wage workers. Permitting the foreign supply conduit to think that the US is full to the brink of illegal people would not induce more to come to America to accept lower and lower wages. Is anybody in government honest today? Let's save that for another book!

In 2002, John McCain estimated that at least ten thousand a day and over 4 million illegal interlopers a year cross the US Southern Border. The 11 million and the McCain estimate of the yearly crossings are clearly out of synch. I go with McCain on this estimate.

Other estimates around the same time were more like 3 million crossings per year. Nobody had ever bothered counting visa overstayers as part of the problem. That is why I have great confidence that the number of illegal interlopers in the country today is 60 million and nowhere close to 11 million.

All Americans know from the rising school populations, crowding in supermarkets, malls, etc., that there are many more migrants than there once were in America despite the official lies suggesting that the number is still 11 million. The promulgators of such false information should be arrested and jailed.

Just as the size of the illegal alien population can only be estimated, and nobody knows for sure, the number of illegal aliens working in the United States is also subject to non-fact-based estimates. A large share of the illegal alien population is generally accepted as being in the workforce because getting some gold in America is what motivates most preparing interlopers to commit the crime of illegal immigration.

However, in the numbers estimates, there are some family members, especially children of illegal aliens who are not in the labor force, while others may be in prison. One recent estimate by researchers at the Pew Hispanic Center puts the number of illegal aliens in the workforce at 8 million out of an overall population of 11.2 million illegal aliens, i.e., 71.4 percent.

That estimate is generally accepted as reasonable. Not by me. I'll take the 71.4 percent number and then when I multiply it by 60 million interlopers in the US today. the total becomes 43 million illegal foreign nationals with jobs in the US that Americans do not have.

Today's immigration system is dysfunctional because it is not responsive to the socioeconomic conditions of the country. In simple terms, our "honorable" politicians do not consider what is good for Americans when forming immigration policy. They go with their donors and the needs of the Democratic Party. All things being equal, not one illegal alien should have a job if one American citizen, who is willing to work, is unemployed.

Only a small share of legally admitted immigrants is sponsored by employers while the bulk are admitted because of family reunification. I am not the only human, who looks at things logically, who fully understands that family reunification is the biggest immigration farce and fraud of all time.

FAIRUS.ORG writes that illegal interlopers often live in poverty or near poverty and tying in family members from abroad to that mix contributes to an already-existing surplus of low-skilled workers. "Do Gooders" make things worse for everybody by doing what the slave traders did years ago—effectively bringing in more slaves. This of course increases job competition and drives down wages and conditions to the detriment of potential American employees, who are not Americans as well as those who are Americans.

The presence of a large illegal workforce perpetuates a vicious cycle. Degraded work conditions discourage Americans accustomed to a livable wage from seeking these jobs and it therefore makes employers more dependent on an illegal foreign workforce. America's massive low-skill labor force and illegal alien population allow employers to create a fast race to the bottom of the wage scale, offering low pay and deplorable conditions.

Meanwhile the employers are making a killing off the backs of the poor with the backing of the "Do-Gooders." Together, they assure that few have sweet dreams of America, a one-time land of prosperity.

Conditions for America's poorest workers continue to deteriorate because of both illegal and legal immigration. Reform of the immigration system to assure that it does not harm Americans and instead contributes to a stronger more equitable society is long overdue. The Pay-to-Go program reduces the number of illegal interlopers, which will in turn have the effect of increasing the wages that greedy employers must pay to gain employees in an open market.

The Resident Visa Plan solves the problem for those interlopers who choose not to leave America and hope things can get better. By having a Resident Visa, they can keep their jobs, which more than likely will soon pay higher wages. Additionally, they swear off welfare and they promise to accept being second choice behind any qualified American citizen for any new job.

They also promise not to ever vote in US elections as a non-citizen. They are not second-class citizens. They have no citizen rights. Instead, with a Resident Visa, they have found a way to stay in America as a temporary resident who can renew their visa every year for eternity. In an economy on the upswing, without millions coming in each year, they ought to do well.

What about Green Card Holders & DACA?

Moreover, as part of the Resident Visa Program, there is a plan to reduce the taxpayer cost for Green card holders, and anchor birthright citizens. It would be 100% voluntary and could result in large stipend payments for those who are interested in Pay-to-Go as well as those who would be fine living in the US with a Resident Visa rather than either being a citizen or a green card holder.

There would be no need for DACA and Dreamers as everybody's opportunity for being legal would be on the table. There would also be no need for sanctuary cities. Everybody's wages would go up with the implementation of the Resident Visa. Businesses could no longer execute labor arbitrage using illegal aliens or the big shot owners would be spending a lot of time in jail.

Besides ending family-based chain migration, the reforms that are needed must decrease unskilled immigration, and end the job competition for America's most vulnerable citizens. Law enforcement must hold employers accountable for hiring illegal workers. They know what they are doing and they do it anyway because it profits them substantially. It won't after a Pay-to-Go and a Resident Visa program is implemented. And, these bad guys might wind up in jail. Say a prayer.

Chapter 12 The Jobs Impact of Illegal Aliens on Black Americans

Effects on Blacks worse than Whites

The Jobs effects of illegal immigration is worse on Black employees. There are many who are prepared to give illegal interlopers as minorities a bigger break than they would be willing to give for similar perpetrations by American citizens. Unfortunately, some of the biggest losers when this mindset is in play are other minorities, such as hard-working Black American employees.

The United States Commission on Civil Rights put out a report on April 4, 2008 titled: *The Impact of Illegal Immigration on the Wages and Employment Opportunities of Black Workers*. The Commission collected the evidence for economic loss and job opportunity costs to black workers attributable to illegal immigration. The panelists also described non-economic factors contributing to the depression of black wages and employment rates.

Based on the facts discovered for this report, the Commission noted that the number of illegal workers has tended to increase the supply of low-skilled, low-wage labor available. Evidence for the negative effects of wage competition against Black Americans ranged from modest to significant, according to the experts who testified.

Even those who viewed the effects as modest overall still found significant effects in occupations such as meatpacking and construction. The wages in these industries have become so depressed because illegal foreign nationals will almost work for nothing, that black opportunities no longer include wages commensurate with the middle class. Check out the fine essay on the next page by Ian Smith:

BY IAN M. SMITH —08/29/16 03:00 PM EDT

Ian M. Smith, for The Hill, on August 29, 2016 discussed the negative effects of illegal immigrants on black employability:

Aamplifiewrote:

In 1994, the majority of blacks in California voted for prop 187; the citizen referendum that ended public benefits to illegal aliens before it was overturned by a federal court judge. Those voters weren't stupid. As the Atlantic *observed at the time, "even if these communities (blacks and Hispanics) make common political cause, do they have any choice about economic competition?" "The almost total absence", the magazine wrote, "of black gardeners, busboys, chambermaids, nannies, janitors, and construction workers in a city with a notoriously large pool of unemployed, unskilled black people leaps to the eye." Things haven't got any better since.*

In the fifty years since our current mass immigration system was created, the black experience has been one of continued shattered hope. Studying census-data from around 1965 (when immigration became dramatically expanded) to 2000, economist Gordon Hanson found that a 10 percent immigrant-induced increase in the labor supply is associated with a 4 percent reduction in both the black wage and employment rates. Between 1980 and 2000, immigration accounted for about 40 percent of the overall 18 percent decline in black employment rates as well as half the 20-percentage point increase in the incarceration rate of black high school dropouts. Similar findings have been found by economists Andrew Sum, George Borjas, and Harry Holzer.

Immigration's negative trickle-down effect on black America doesn't end there. Immigration economist Vernon Briggs has written a lot on how the worsening situation for black laborers, mostly males, passes onto their households and affects the entire social structure of black society. Today, almost half of black women ages 25-44 are not married compared to 15 percent of white women; a fact, he writes, that's no doubt partly due to the increasing difficulty black men have in finding a traditional standard of living in an overcrowded labor market.

Such concentration also puts stress on urban schools. Per-pupil spending decreases greatly as bilingual programs and special education classes for underprepared Latin American students work to divert resources. Then there's affirmative action. With the Hispanic population (including illegal aliens) soon to double that of blacks the slots available to the latter in set-aside programs, colleges, and public employment must shrink. *It's as if the beginning of our modern mass immigration system in 1965 evaporated the pent-up gains from the civil rights struggle.*

FAIR sums up the plight of black workers and others who have been negatively affected by illegal immigration. Americans are not second class citizens of the world. Americans deserve decent jobs and decent wages. They did not ask politicians to create unfair competition using imported foreign workers, who are so afraid of their situation that they permit themselves to be exploited to the point of indentured servitude.

There is no question that we need real immigration reform to stop the massive influx of foreign workers from harming the living standard of our most vulnerable citizens. The Pay-to-Go program and the Resident Visa Program are designed to help even the score and then tilt the balance in favor of US citizens, whether black or white or yellow.

Meatpacking has always been a terrible industry in which to work. The raw materials in many cases are live animals and the finished product is always dead and often frozen. What happens in-between can turn even a strong-man's stomach.

As the US was figuring out what it was as a country, people had to eat, and meat was a great source of protein as it still is. Entrepreneurs in the meatpacking industry were never interested in giving away the store in wages and so they always sought the cheapest labor possible.

Other than freed slaves in the late 19th century, the original slaughterhouse workers were largely recent immigrants of Irish, German, and Scandinavian background. Not only were they required to slaughter and dismember enormous numbers of animals each day, the rest of the working conditions were also very poor.

The employees were exposed to poor environmental conditions, including leaks of contaminated water, liquid waste and sewage across the floors. The shops were poorly lit and the rooms were cold. Injuries and illnesses were commonplace among workers. It often did not get better when the workers went home. Most lived in slums next to the slaughterhouses.

They were ripe for unionization but it did not come for another 50 years. In the early 1880s, workers called for higher wages and better working conditions. The bosses would have none of it. and the owners used their ethnic differences to maintain control. It was easy to find recent immigrants who were willing to work such as vulnerable Poles, Serbs, Croatians, Slovaks, and other recent Southern and Eastern European immigrants all wanted to be employed for any amount.

Eventually, these mostly white workers were able to organize and go on strike in 1894. Instead of giving in at the time, slaughterhouse owners began recruiting African-American workers to break the strike.

The slaughterhouse was always a place of blood and stench and danger and it was like that for most of the 19th century. But it was mostly a local thing with butchers commanding top dollar as skilled craftsmen. The idea of large meatpacking houses did not take hold until after 1860 because it was almost impossible to ship meats across the country unrefrigerated. Once the refrigerated railcar was invented, things changed and the meatpacking industry quickly came into being and the entrepreneurs were in charge of everything.

Unions eventually came to meatpacking but not right away. It was not until the Congress of Industrial Organizations (CIO) organized the workers. The National Labor Relations Act in 1935 also helped in improving working conditions for slaughterhouse workers, but it never got really good—the nature of the job.

In 1909, only 1% of the meatpacking workforce was black but as white workers demanded more and more, especially higher and higher wages, black workers took up the slack until 1929 when 30% of the meatpackers were black. By the time illegal alien workers began to dominate the industry, black workers were the dominant force, and they too unionized and forced the hands of the meatpacker owners to pay a middle class wage.

Unfortunately, Americans, born black or white in America, know that wages as a whole in America have gone down substantially for many years, as the scum of the entrepreneurial class have preferred to hire illegal foreign nationals as workers for slave wages to maximize profits rather than sharing a bit of their bounty with those who helped produce it.

In the meatpacking industry, once dominated by unionized black workers as noted—people who had worked their way out of poverty and well into the middle class over the years—once earned as much as $20.00 per hour in the late 1980's. Blacks in meatpacking had great lives with great salaries.

Blacks more than anybody became the victims of liberal interpretations of our immigration laws. They saw their average wages fall to just over $9.00 per hour as non-union illegal foreign national workers took over their jobs and in fact the illegals agreed to move from Chicago and other big cities to places where nobody but illegal workers lived.

How did this happen. When companies moved from the big cities and built "worker cities," most regular Americans chose not to move. This action did not help black or white workers. If big business people were honest about what happened, they would say that lowering the wages and hiring illegal workers did not help the employees and it was not intended to do so. t sure helped the bottom line of the profiteers, however. The average wage in meatpacking, now dominated by illegal aliens, is substantially less than in other manufacturing areas.

Case Farms, for example, built its business by recruiting immigrant workers, some of the world's most vulnerable, from Guatemala. They are still forced to endure conditions, at times illegal conditions that few Americans would put up with. Big companies have gotten really bold in trying to squeeze out more profits on the backs of hard-luck immigrants whose wages keep going down. Blacks and whites are mostly out of meatpacking due to the malleability of illegal foreign workers.

Tyson Foods Inc., the nation's largest meat producer and processor, was indicted way back in 2001 with six employees on charges that it conspired to smuggle illegal immigrants across the Mexican border to work in its processing plants. How many do you think were successful? Big Business and the Democratic Party love illegal residents even if it hurts the interloper and those citizens who the Democrats are counting as yes votes.

Bringing in poor, uneducated, people from south of the border, often criminals, who feed from our welfare system, taking tax dollars from those with minimal incomes, assures the Democratic politicians of the illegal's votes for a long time once they are in America. Who pays for these illegal aliens?

It is the working slobs such as you and I, who happen to pay taxes, who pay for them. Black employees who made big wages in meatpacking paid for them by having to give up their nice jobs. Yes, there is no coming back for these poor black folks who twenty-years ago were once making $20.00 an hour in a meatpacking job and now with no union protection from illegal workers, if they chose to stay employed would have to work in a non-union shop for $8.00 or $9.00 per hour in the same job if they could get it.

Mostly black Americans, who labored for the big wages in the meatpacking industry of yore, had a choice to work for $8.00 or $9.00 per hour if they did not complain. They did not have the option, however, to keep the $20.00 per hour wage that they had won in prior Union negotiations. The unions were gone.

Their other choice was not to work in meatpacking. Nobody in government was protecting the American wage v the illegal foreign national wage. Nobody even talked about the fact that under the covers of the flag, such nasty labor arbitrage with foreigners was occurring.

American businesses love paying the smallest wage possible and since illegal foreign nationals work for peanuts, there has been a perfect marriage of needs.

In summary, illegal immigration has had a disproportionately negative effect on the wages and employment levels of blacks, particularly black males. The huge number of illegal immigrants ensures that there is a continual surplus of low-skilled labor, thus preventing black wages from rising. Not only do illegal immigrants compete for jobs with African-Americans, but that competition drives down wages for all of the jobs that are available.

The US needs no more immigration until wages come back to a level that normal Americans will accept.

Chapter 13 Other Cultural / Social Issues

The impact of illegal aliens on healthcare

Besides education as previously discussed, healthcare, and incarceration are without a doubt, the three main social services that are used by illegal aliens in the United States to sustain themselves. I suspect that none of them are happy about gaining their sustenance from the three squares in a prison, but in some cases, it may beat working when food is not guaranteed.

Researching the topic, it is easy to find that in 1996, the Illegal Immigration Reform and Immigrant Responsibility Act (IIRIRA) was created. It did not look kindly on Americans picking up the tab for services of any kind provided for foreigners. Likewise, Americans, who travel abroad, should not expect to have a free ride on the people of every other country in the world where they choose to visit.

The 1996 USA Law banned most public services to illegal immigrants, but it allowed illegal immigrants to access "emergency" medical services and provide pregnant women and infants with care (especially since most of these infants are U.S. citizens via a misinterpretation of the 14th amendment)

As you would expect, immigrants are often either uninsured or underinsured. The best stats I could find suggested that forty-three percent of noncitizens under 65 have no health insurance. That means that in the 1990's, there were 9.4 million uninsured immigrants, a majority of whom were in the country illegally.

This constituted 15 percent of the total uninsured in the nation in the mid-1990s. The cost of the medical care of these uninsured immigrants is always passed onto the taxpayer, and it strains the financial stability of the health care community.

Another problem is immigrants' use of hospital and emergency services using EMTALA rather than preventative medical care. For example, utilization rate of hospitals and clinics by illegal aliens (29 percent) is more than twice the rate of the overall U.S. population (11 percent). Visit an emergency room and you will see this in action.

As a result, the costs of medical care for immigrants are staggering. The estimated cost of unreimbursed medical care in 2004 in California was about $1.4 billion per year. In Texas, the estimated cost was about $.85 billion, and in Arizona the comparable estimate was $.4 billion per year. Despite that no Democrat inclined judge in the US is willing to say enough—pay your own way.

One of the frequent costs to U.S. taxpayers is delivery of babies to illegal alien mothers. A California study put the number of these anchor baby deliveries in the state in 1994 at 74,987, at a cost of $215 million. The US number approaches 400,000 babies per year. Each becomes a permanent welfare citizen until they reach 18 and then it is up to them to get a job or not. This is not fair to normal Americans.

At that time in CA, those California births constituted 36 percent of all Medi-Cal births, and they have grown now to substantially more than half of the annual Medi-Cal budget. In 2003, 70 percent of the 2,300 babies born in San Joaquin General Hospital's maternity ward were anchor babies.

They may decide to pay nothing but their healthcare is not free. Medi-Cal in 2003 had 760,000 illegal alien beneficiaries, up from 2002, when there were 470,000. US statistics such as these for recent years are hard to come by as the government really does not want us to know the truth.

Incarceration as a social service.

When Americans commit a crime, and go to jail to make amends for their infractions, it can be argued their meals are not free. They have paid the taxes necessary for their incarceration including the guards, and the meals and the facility maintenance crews. They are not good guys. They are bad guys who were masquerading as good guys until they were caught and sent to jail. I have no pity on them other than their immortal souls.

So, why would anybody think that if a foreigner in the US illegally commits a crime, they should not pay their due. That's the rub. Illegal immigrants who commit crimes in the Unites States are either released as in sanctuary cities, or they fill up spots in various lock-ups all paid for by people who contribute to the US tax system. There is no free lunch—even in prison. But like everything else, the illegal interlopers do not contribute.

Incarceration is the last social service that illegal immigrants, specifically those who commit crimes, are taking advantage of. And, unfortunately, they do, and they think our providing a roof, three squares, clean clothes, etc. is just another one of their many rights.

President Trump is a very smart man. He worked for his gains, just like you worked for yours and I worked for mine. He represents all of us and President Trump is not going to let those who think illegal foreign nationals have more rights than Americans have any legitimate claim to that idea. Trump plans to shut them all down at the pass.

His Department of Justice on a Tuesday in May 2017, released its first set of data on the incarceration rates of undocumented immigrants ordered by the President in an effort to build a case for more aggressive enforcement of immigration laws. Why did we wait so long? Answer: Congress is working for anti-American forces. Let's look at what they said:

Of the 45,493 foreign-born inmates in the federal prison system made up of 188,658 inmates, the Justice Department said 3,939 are U.S. citizens. What does this really mean?

According to the agency data, immigration orders have been issued for 54.2 percent — about 22,541 — of the remaining 41,554 incarcerated immigrants. Why do Americans have to pay to babysit thugs from other countries? Ask your Congress.

Another 33.4 percent, about 13,886 inmates, are under investigation by U.S. Immigration and Customs Enforcement for possible removal.

The Justice Department said about 12.3 percent — or 5,101 — of the illegal immigrants behind bars are still waiting adjudication and 26 have been granted relief because they risk persecution or serious harm if they are deported.

Why is this type of information in this chapter? Well, because citizens all want to solve the problem despite the fact that politicians still have not figured out that they represent Americans and not illegal foreign nationals.

If politicians represented Americans, once they heard about the Pay-to-Go and the Resident Visa Plan, they would do handstands to get the legislation enacted. Nobody knows who they represent. So, we better rid ourselves of them.

It is difficult to separate the financial issues involved in illegal immigration social issues and the major costs to US taxpayers from those of a non-financial nature, as they do most certainly intertwine. There are two sides to every story. In these cases, there are those who think America is great and there are those who think America is the cause of every problem.

Read more at:
http://www.nationalreview.com/corner/447267/federal-prison-illegal-immigrants-taxpayers-pay-about-12-billion

Costs and Benefits

Americans are very concerned about rapid migrations

Few issues are more controversial for Americans than immigration. Those fortunate enough to be living in gated communities, such as our friendly Congress-Persons, are far removed from the social problems. The stay far away intentionally so they can have an excuse for failing to see the true effects of what is happening. Therefore, they tend to be more generous in their perceptions regarding the foreign perpetrators and less generous in their good-will towards normal Americans.

Nonetheless, the massive flood of illegal immigrants across U.S. borders continues to enrage many native-born residents who believe that immigrants compete for jobs, unfairly draw on government benefits, and fundamentally alter the social fabric of America.

These native-borns fear that non-English-speaking foreigners who move to the United States—legally or illegally—and do not integrate into mainstream social and political life, threaten to erase American culture's distinctive character. Part of this anxiety is rooted in ethnocentrism and group animus. But there is evidence to back up their feelings. Yes, it is natural for people not to like others who look or act differently from themselves, especially when their actions cost them in the wallet or in their quality of life.

Many Americans are concerned about immigration because they view the material costs of open-door policies as broad-based but see the benefits as concentrated. The impact of open policies falls on workers whose skills are not unique. They have seen their wages depressed by newcomers when such actions are illogical And, so, taxpayers watch politicians draining public resources to benefits illegal foreign national interlopers and harm American citizens. They see these actions continue unabated without a solution on the horizon.

It is not possible for the American political system, especially with Obama left-overs favoring foreign-borns vs native borns, to resolve the many conflicts involving immigration. Observant taxpayers have noticed that illegal aliens receive more benefits than they deserve and that the social costs of illegal arrivals are enormous.

There is no wonder why the prevailing citizen interpretations are as they are. Americans are suffering because of lax enforcement by public officials. Immigration will remain controversial until it is addressed with lasting solutions that do not cost the taxpayers money. Pay-to-Go is a great start to help round out the score for Americans. Those who won't go can help America by signing up for the Resident Visa. In the end nobody, if Congress acts will be in the shadows or in any sanctuary.

There are many who favor punitive policies as all illegals in America have committed a crime or they would be legal. Political leaders care more about their political parties or their donor base to address the problem head-on. In this book, I completely agree with the predominant feeling in America that US citizens have gotten a raw deal because of a political immigration policy.

There are enough laws on the books to have prevented over 60 million illegal interlopers to be living in the shadows today. Now that they have made their present felt, to clean out the 60 million interlopers, spruce up the green card system, and make the anchor baby system affordable, it is time for Congress to enact the Pay-to-Go program along with the Resident Visa Program.

The fear and anxiety of normal Americans over illegal immigration is legitimate. When there are too many low-skilled foreign nationals for the low-skilled jobs available, the citizens get hurt. There is no need for 60 million illegal immigrants to bring a "brain gain" of innovation and creativity that outweighs the costs of supporting the lives of the illegal aliens.

People from other countries should support themselves, especially people who forced their way into America, or they should self deport or take the Pay-to-Go option or demand a Resident Visa so that the social cost for Americans is not so great and so that the financial cost can be reduced to zero.

It can be argued that in this nation's history, immigrants have enriched economic, intellectual, social, and cultural life in the United States in a number of fundamental respects. But, once the population reached 5 million years ago after the revolution, the country never needed any more than that necessary to fill jobs as the coutnry expanded. The US has not expanded in thirty-years. We need no foreigners to make life miserable for Americans.

When we became a country, the early US patriots knew that they had to take measures to protect America's borders and its people from encroachment by other countries. Of course. Only a dummy would think that opening borders to people who either do not like US or people who would like to kill US makes sense.

Just seven years after the adoption of the US Constitution, the new US government passed the Naturalization Act of 1790 in which it established the rules for naturalized citizenship, as per Article 1, Section 8 of the Constitution. Then to make immigration even more restrictive, the Congress passed the Naturalization Act of 1795 which lengthened required residency to become citizen.

There were more immigration laws passed in 1798. Together these toughened the prior acts. Nobody was asking Congress to water down the idea that immigration needed to be controlled by the US. Because or Congress chose not to assure its laws were executed, they need to be replaced. Americans can do much better than the knaves who hold office today.

The 1798 acts included the extending of the duration of residence required for immigrants to become citizens from five years to 14 years. The acts also authorized the president to deport any resident immigrant considered "dangerous to the peace and safety of the United States." The president was also authorized in 1798 to apprehend and deport resident aliens if their home countries were at war with the United States of America.

Think of the impact of this on the Trump immigration ban. Too bad the spirit of the founders is not operative today within the interpretations of the corrupt judges appointed during the Obama years. This law was enacted July 6, 1798, and it provided no sunset provision. Thus, the act remains intact today as 50 U.S.C. T

The problem of course is that today the US can be at war with a country yet it is not declared, and our Congress today is very weak in regard to protecting Americans. Too bad we could not just give them a toughening pill. I suspect that which their donors provide, in their minds is enough. Since their donors do not work for America or for American Citizens, I would suggest sending this Congress home ashamed and sending their donors to prison on sedition charges. Think about it.

Chapter 14 Interlopers Do Not Have It So Easy In America

A Banana Republic President & Congress

Too bad things are not going well for Americans regarding the items that the illegals are winning every day. If you think you love America and you think you are a long-term loyal American—the type of which would have been a Patriot in the late 1700s—but you were born 2 hundred years too late, you cannot like the decisions Congress and the prior President made on your behalf. Me neither!

There is no apparent reason, at least while reading this book, to pine about a do-nothing Congress and a past president, who for over eight years did everything to hurt normal people regarding the stain of illegal immigration on our shores. We have cobbled up a great solution without this president and we hope we have help from here-on-in. Think Pay-to-Go and Resident Visa as both notions are keys to victory for normal Americans over the transgressors, who you already know.

In many ways, the effect on illegal foreign nationals in the US has been as devastating and almost as much of a cultural shock as poor Africans being stolen in their homeland to come to America to be placed in servitude. Think about it. The last eight years were not good years in American History. They were not good for foreign interlopers in the squalor of the shadows, and they were not good for American citizens living by three-bedroom homes with twenty in residence.

Congress, either by action or by inaction permitted this travesty on the most vulnerable and most hopeful people on earth. Who knows what the African profiteers told the ultimate American slaves as they were forced to get on their ships to America and to Europe. There are too many similarities. And, it is sickening on both accounts.

Greed in both cases is the cause. In these recent past years, US officials have created a scourge on the illegal foreign national population. These interlopers did their jobs by working for barely enough to survive but greed again caused the new age robber barons to exact even a greater toll from their subjects. Illegal foreign nationals often replaced unknowing good-hearted Americans who had no idea what hit them. Poof—No job!

Next thing they knew Americans were out of work or they were forced in order to survive to work under the table for peanuts. How could anybody, knowing the pain so many people experienced, want more of this in our country? Why does nobody with a powerful hand, even a "Do-Gooder," really want to solve this. Shame on politicians! Why do Democrats, who say one thing and do another, want to harm the lives of foreign families by bringing them into the shadow economy of the US? Why do "Do Gooders" condone this?

For Americans, if you add up our outlays to illegal foreign nationals, our treasury has been depleted to feed foreigners while many Americans cannot find proper work to feed themselves. Perhaps it appears selfish while others too, from various countries are suffering, to focus on the treasury drain but this problem exudes a puss from the greed of the new robber barons who cannot be fought in normal terms.

The people's own representatives are infecting the puss against the people. This can be fixed but not by timid people. Americans must toughen up again like at our founding. Dirty scoundrel politicians must be identified, publicized and ostracized

Do the poor all belong in America?

There are a number of countries who have a habit of exporting their poor to America because their country greed causes them to find a sucker to permit them to have another layer on their cakes and another inch on their steaks, and more presents for their children than they could reasonably open in a day.

"Ship the poor to America as those American dummies will put their own people in chains to give us even more profits." Plus, we will never have to look at those wretched half-people ever again. Drink up to the master's health! Drink Up! Enjoy! If it is not that bad, at times, it surely seems that it is.

Figures available in 2012 show the immigrant mix from many areas across the world: 52% were from Mexico, 15% from Central America, 12% from Asia, 6% from South America, 5% from the Caribbean, and another 5% from Europe and Canada.

Of course, it is right and proper for Americans to decide not to be chumps for these areas of the world. We don't even get help from our leaders. There are way too many traitorous American representatives asking us to turn our backs on their greed. No more!

Stop the treasury drain!

The best way to stop the treasury drain is to send all the treasury sucking politicians back home. We must stand up and no longer take it just like we stood up and threw out lousy candidates for president in 2016. We are now forced to replace almost the entire Congress in order to do the right thing for America. Who will be the first good man to say let's adopt the Pay-to-Go and the Resident Visa programs? If we are waiting for Congress to act, we will hear nothing I fear.

If a resident illegal foreign national really does not want to go home regardless of the incentive, then under the proposed plan, there is another option that again costs taxpayers nothing and permits the interloper to stay in America indefinitely in a legal state as long as they "behave."

Our greedy Congress more than likely will not like this either as it will result in higher wages for Americans. This is unlikely to please political donors who like slave level wages. Let's not let the Congress stop us. Instead, we must identify them by their resistance so we can deliver their walking papers.

Resident Visa can change America for the better

Americans are willing to help these poor souls from foreign countries if for no other reason that they were lured here by a corrupt Congress, who would do anything to please their donors. But Congress may not want to help. Congress either must come kicking and screaming to the table of reasonableness or they should show us all that their bags are packed and they are ready to go. We the people will pay the freight to ship them home one last time.

For those interlopers who do not want to take the money and go home (Pay-to-Go), the new program provides for granting interlopers in good standing a *Resident Visa*.

This is a new visa type that, unlike other visa types can be renewed each year. With this visa, former foreign nationals would be legal under the protection of the Resident Visa and could remain in America as long as they behave in a lawful manner according to the exact terms of their new visa.

There are many differences between illegally gaining benefits in the United States and becoming legal by gaining a Resident Visa. Those choosing to employ the Resident Visa to stay in America, are welcome to do so if approved; but the terms of the relationship with US officials will not be the same as when they were in illegal status. For example, there will be no more cash incentives. There will be no welfare. There will be no more free-medical- care. Everything that a resident visa holder gets would come out of their wallet.

For those very familiar with the notion of American visas, this unique visa permits those approved to live in America as long as they want. To gain this benefit, they must renew their Resident Visa each and every year. In essence, this process provides a Resident Visa, an official temporary US Visa, which provides all of the benefits of a US non-immigrant category visa and more.

Will liberal progressive Democrats and the press bad-mouth the plan?

I think we can count on Democrats finding fault with anything that does not keep interlopers in chains living in the shadows and /or the Democrat controlled sanctuaries across the country—unless, of course they are able to vote. Democrats will say the plan makes second-class citizens of the illegal aliens and therefore it is not good. Of course, they will be wrong as it frees them to lead a normal life in America.

The liberal progressive ideology has a habit of taking words and making their usage appear to be, for want of a better word, *bad.* There is nothing intrinsically wrong with the word *illegal*, and there is nothing intrinsically wrong with the word, *alien*.

Moreover, when the term illegal alien, as used in US immigration law, is used in everyday speech, there is nothing implied that makes the term disrespectful to the person who fits the description. It is merely a statement of fact that permits an individual to be identified and described with accuracy without caring about their name.

What is US law's meaning of *illegal alien*

1. a foreigner who has entered or resides in a country unlawfully or without the country's authorization.
2. a foreigner who enters the U.S. without an entry or immigrant visa, especially a person who crosses the border by avoiding inspection or who overstays the period of time allowed as a visitor, tourist, or businessperson.

I hope nobody is upset by these facts as used by US immigration authorities for the very first laws on immigration.

Illegal alien, *illegal*, *undocumented*, and *unauthorized* are various labels used to describe people who have chosen to unlawfully reside in the United States, whether because of a clandestine border crossing, visa deadline violation, or other means. But these terms as defined by liberal progressives are not interchangeable. Each has a unique origin and connotation.

Alien for example, is a term used in legal language for a noncitizen resident, regardless of whether that person resides in the country legally or illegally. The term in the United States is inherited from British law, and has had a legal designation for foreign-born residents since the Revolutionary era.

While the term continues to be used by the Department of Homeland Security and the United States Immigration and Customs Enforcement as a technical term in legal documents, leftists (progressive liberals) in America have made the term volatile and for their discourse it is not preferred. However, non-leftists find the term perfectly OK.

Though the terms *illegal immigrant* and *illegal resident* may have an anti-immigration connotation to leftists with an anti-American agenda, it is still largely accepted as proper.

The left likes to rework words for its own purposes and they are all about feeling good rather than fact. They do not care if Americans feel good but they go out of their way so that illegal aliens feel really good and are not offended by being called what they legally are: *illegal aliens.*

To the left it is more sensitive to use the convoluted terms undocumented or unauthorized when describing these people, but this is not technically all that illegal and alien mean.

US immigration law uses the term illegal alien and does not waiver. The left has gone berserk in wordsmithing perfectly acceptable clear meaning words into unclear agenda-perfect words. Sometimes people actually get fired for not using the correct word or phrase. The left operates a dangerous game with words that only avowed leftists can fully comprehend.

Since we are suggesting that Congress create a brand-new visa category—Resident Visa--one might get the idea that there are thousands of US visa categories and that I am suggesting just one more. Not true! There are only two visa types today, and there will be just three when the Resident Visa is fully approved.

What types of visas are there?

The type of visa that a visitor or traveler must obtain is defined by U.S. immigration law, and relates to the purpose of the travel. There is one new category of visa proposed for current illegal alien US residents in addition to the two main categories of existing U.S. visas:

1. **Nonimmigrant visas**– For travel to the United States on a temporary basis.
2. **Immigrant visas**–For travel to live permanently in the United States.
3. **Resident visas**–New-- For current resident aliens to live temporarily in the US on an annually renewable basis.

Description of the new visa category

Under the new Resident Visa Program, a third type of visa would be authorized by US officials. It is called a Resident Visa. Current law says all visa holders must first have passports containing information such as their home country and other pertinent information. As other visas, the new visa category will also require a pre-existing passport.

The new visa category is intended for those residents formerly in an illegal status who register for and are granted a Resident Visa. Unlike other visas, the Resident Visa may be renewed annually as long as the holder does not violate the terms of the visa.

Like all visa requests, the individual must first possess a passport and then apply for the Resident Visa. The costs for the resident passport and the Resident Visa would be the same as under current law. An additional charge may be added to the visa fee for an ID card so the Resident Visa holder does not have to keep the passport and visa on their person at all times.

The Visa as proposed would be renewable annually for a fee between $100 and $200 to reflect changes such as address or marital status etc. The ID card and photo and changeable biometric scans, if any, would be required to be refreshed every five years.

Since the new program in its entirety would provide for the voluntary egress of illegal aliens (Pay-to-Go) as well as Resident Visas for those who choose to stay in America, this is a combination plan. An interloper would get to execute just one of the two options.

The part of this plan that most Americans will want to learn more about to assure that they are getting a fair shake is the Resident Visa Program. The Pay-to-Go Plan is fairly self-explanatory. My opinion is that it will remain the quiet part of this revolutionary program. Despite its serendipitous presence, it will save the US the most treasury tax dollars.

At the end of the day that Congress passes this legislation and the President signs it, the United States will have no more resident aliens. There will be no more shadows; there will be no more DACA, and there will be no more sanctuary cities as they will no longer be "needed."

Can you imagine how positive that will be for all Americans and former interlopers alike. Instead, the former foreign interlopers will either have gained a Resident Visa and be legalized and be under the terms of the visa or they will be in their home countries cashing their massive stipend checks from Pay-to-Go, while preparing to knock them dead as entrepreneurs in their home countries.

No treat for illegal interlopers to live in America

Liberal progressives are kidding themselves when they think they are helping illegal aliens remain in this country. For most, living in the shadows and earning sub-minimum wages is like living in a hell-hole, hidden from the rest of America. When an interloper leaves the safety of the shadows today, their hearts beat ten beats faster.

Everybody knows that illegal aliens live as residents in the shadows, fearful of being seen by authorities for the continual fear of deportation. The shadows are America's poorest neighborhoods. Often, illegal aliens are forced to live in abject squalor.

Worse than that, they are treated as sewer-rats by the government and the liberal do-gooders who encourage them to come to America, promising them the world, while caring only for their votes. How do-gooders can feel good after delivering excrement sandwiches to these hard luck souls is a puzzle for many good people.

The businesses for which illegal foreign nationals work use the nastiest forms of labor arbitrage to trick the interlopers into working for slave wages without complaining. Nobody is saying slavery is or was ever good. However, it is undeniable that the slaves were fed, if for no other reason than to keep them strong and healthy so their output would be optimal.

Today's illegal aliens are on their own and they have a hard time finding enough wages to be able to eat enough to live. It is no treat living in the shadows of America.

Anybody thinking that illegal aliens are having a daily picnic on American taxpayer expense are way off the mark for what is really happening. I say this without denying that supporting the meager existence of 60 million illegal interlopers requires quite a bit if US resources and over time if we do not address it well, it will bankrupt US.

Big Business knows what it is doing. It has a great financial deal paying scant wages for top work. It is cheating American laws and American citizens by hiring illegal foreign nationals to get work done on the cheap. They often do not pay even the minimum wage and they never pay the prevailing wage. If they paid the prevailing wage, think about it; they would not demand that the US Chamber of Commerce threaten Republicans into voting for amnesty.

American citizens are not attracted to such low-wage jobs; but worse than that, illegal foreign nationals are lured from their home countries, risking everything they know and love, thinking they are going to a better life. They quickly find that the big fat cats get the benefit of their labor without paying them a fair wage.

In his or her heart, the illegal foreign national worker knows they are in America illegally. They will do almost anything to not be discovered by others or turned in by their employers if they fail to produce.

They live in the shadows with others of their ilk and they accept their plight because their only other choice is to leave the country to conditions that are perhaps even worse. Pay-to-Go may help many of these and the Resident Visa will help all the others who chose to stay in America.

They know the dirty clandestine rules. And, so they accept wages that barely put food on their tables. Would fair-thinking Americans not be better off paying such victims stipends in their home countries rather than handing American fat cat businessmen the opportunity to exploit their labor and make their lives utterly miserable?

The US extends foreign aid in the amount of just over $50 billion in total to countries who do far less for America than feed their citizens and make sure they have no need to come to America. We might do well to add $50 billion to direct a national endowment to help people in their home countries not require illegal passage to America to survive. The shadows surely are not what any foreigner would expect as the reward for arriving in America.

Considering that the current cost to America is about $500 billion per year to as much as $1 Trillion a year. We get to pay this every year by not solving the resident illegal foreign national crisis. This of course has created a financial crisis which begs for an immediate solution. The Pay-to-Go along with the Resident Visa were made to solve the problem for America and Americans.

Paying to help people in their home countries is a far more charitable and economically beneficial idea than luring them into America to gain their vote or put them to work for peanuts. Why didn't Congress think of that? Could it be that Congress would not please their lobbyist's firms who advocate for cheap labor? Is our Congress that corrupt?

Who would really want to travel in danger from home to the Bronx, or Scranton, PA, or Podunk, IA, or Bloomfield NJ, when they can have a fine life in their home country. What if the US gave them a big hunk of money to go back?

Americans are not really happy about the 60,000,000 illegals living in the shadows. The press says this new batch of "immigrants" are not like our parents. They are not willing to even take a crack at assimilating in the US and melting into the melting pot. Why should we be surprised when the same press mocks America at every opportunity.

I am an American. I love America and that is why I wrote this book.

We are OK helping people. We just don't want anybody, whether a foreign interloper or an American hard on their luck, looking for an easier life, to be able to get that life simply by sticking their hand in, let's say, our pockets. How would that be fair? What would that teach anybody?

Nobody who I know hates the illegal alien population but many Americans are well aware that the benefits that are accrued to dirty businesses are one way. They hire these poor souls and they exploit them for all they have. They take the best they have to offer while returning to them a mere pittance from their efforts.

It is a simple matter of human greed over human goodness. Why don't reporters report the names of the people in business who hurt so many foreign nationals who want nothing more than a better life. Why are the NFL players not working to make sure neither blacks nor whites nor illegal aliens are hurt by corporate greed?

Let me be clear, however. The interlopers are more than half of the problem. If they did not crash our borders through physical travel or via Student Visa or H-1B visa or other visa over-stays, this would not be the best-selling book that it is destined to be.

Americans simply no longer want to be chumps. We'd love to help people in their home countries for $50 billion a year rather than pay

$500 billion to $1 Trillion each year for taking care of them in America. Can we make a deal for that? What do you say?

Wage impact

Unfortunately, Americans, born black or white, know that wages as a whole in America have gone down substantially as the scum of the entrepreneurial class have preferred to hire illegal foreign nationals as workers for slave wages to maximize profits rather than sharing a bit of their bounty with those who helped produce it. We can solve this problem by adopting the Pay-to-Go and the Resident Visa.

American citizens have been played for chumps by the big business tycoons and the vote-seeking dirty politicians in the progressive Democratic Party. If there was enough for everybody, Americans would not be complaining.

While the average wage has been going down, big business, backed by the US Chamber of Congress have put America through the same labor arbitrage as when the Robber Barons chose to take it all at the end of the 19th century. You may recall reading in the history books about many Americans, who had to work most of a 24-hour day in order to barely feed their families.

Family reunification has become a dirty word

Americans do not want to hear the words family reunification ever again. The best place for family reunification for illegal aliens is in their home country. The whole family can live there in peace. It is tough enough to absorb the illegal aliens themselves into the US welfare state with free education, free healthcare, and free this and free that. At the same time, daughters and sons of Americans are not as fortunate in the welfare game, simply because they are not illegal aliens.

American big shots on the charity scene seem to want to help those here illegally, but for some strange reason, they have disdain for American citizens. They do not have the same charitable instincts to help John and Jane Doe of Regular America. Americans do not want charity. That is a fact. However, we do not want our taxes to pay for others who should have to work as hard as we do to survive.

Nobody wants to be a sucker and nobody wants to be a chump; but corrupt American politicians have no problem dealing from the bottom of the deck for regular Americans.

Liberal progressives are always more generous with other people's dollars then their own. The point is that there are many Americans, who have it tougher than those illegal interlopers living in the shadows. Nobody is taking care of Americans or we would at least have first crack at all jobs and nobody would be able to work for sub-minimum wages. Jesus said, "the poor you will always have with you..." Illegal aliens must bear the consequences of their own migration decisions rather than be asking US taxpayers to bail them out with ill-gotten welfare so they can live in America for free.

The Resident Visa program does solve the problem for Americans and illegal foreign nationals. A mom with a baby might cost taxpayers about $300,000 over a five-year period. The Pay-to-Go program can be a great solution as the full stipend for two would be $40,000. That would go a long way in the home country.

In five years the US treasury would save $260,000 and the young family with a child citizen would have more than enough cash to go home to their own country and be reunited with all their family members, including the dad. Americans like that kind of family reunification—in the interloper's home country.

Since an anchor baby has many more rights as a citizen than a baby brought to the US, I would suggest a $50,000 stipend for anchor babies, no matter how old they may be. For a mom and a baby in that case, they would receive $70,000 in Pay-to-Go stipends. They then could start new lives with a nice nest-egg at home in their own home-town, not in the shadows of somebody else's town.

Add those who cross the border illegally to the visa over-stayers, and it is no wonder whole communities in the US have already sprung up in which over 90% of the residents are foreign interlopers. Since 1986 (to 2017 -- 32 years), the time of the massive Reagan amnesty, if we were to use john McCain's famous estimated rate of 4 million new illegal interlopers per year, the total number in the US would amount to 4 X 32 = 128 million. That is an awful lot of people with way too many on the US welfare dole.

Should everybody come to America?

Some say that the US should have open borders? Ask them how much they are willing to contribute out of their own pockets when a human being is declared legal and citizen-like and thus eligible legally for the minimum $30,000 in benefits to which they immediately become entitled. The wallets of the do-gooders' are always hidden when it comes time to help. Normal Americans foot the bill.

Yet, the illegal community gets bonanzas regularly from politicians, hoping one day to get their vote and from a Congress that hopes their actions will please the donor class to assure their reelections. Political corruption is now the law, not the exception in America.

Out of the almost 7 billion people in the world, there are approximately 3 billion people, who are for their own reasons, not too pleased with their home countries. Low-ball estimates suggest that of these 3 billion, there are from 500,000,000 to 1,000,000,000 ready to come to America immediately, as soon as we open our borders. More would surely follow until we closed the spigot.

With 325 million people residing in the US today, and already most not able to find a parking space, let alone a job, can you imagine how crowded it would be if the whole world were to choose to relocate to the US.

To what country would the US be able to go to in order to get some financial relief so we would be able to afford the equipment and personnel to bulldoze government lands and our national parks so we could build all the tent cities necessary to house the portion of the 3 billion people who would come to the US tomorrow if they could.

If they come, can we be assured that they will behave well? So far, no other country has been motivated to step up to help us if the world decides to relocate to America. Unlike the decisions of our Congress, the concerns of leaders in other countries is apparently for their own citizens.

The solution in this book that is concurrently being sent to the US government, addresses the matter completely, effectively, and fairly. I am a Democrat but this solution is just as appropriate for Republicans, Independents, and others. It is the product of copious research and a lot of thinking.

As noted previously, it is a Pay-to-Go program that includes a Resident Visa Program for those who would prefer to live in America out of the shadows and sanctuaries. I would suggest that it should be passed and implemented ASAP. The problem with 60 million illegal interlopers in residence in the US would be solved instantly.

There would be no more sub-minimum wages for anybody, and Americans would be first for jobs. One million criminals would be able to be deported. There would be no more anchor babies and no more sanctuary cities and no more $500 Billion to $1 Trillion payments for supporting the 60 million illegal aliens in the US.

Americans are always first in this plan. Moreover, it is not a denigrating notion to future Resident Visa Holders, who like other types of temporary visa holders, are not citizens but are temporary guests of *our country*.

Visa holders are "visitors;" not citizens

When you have guests in your own home, you still control your property. You do not let your guests do whatever they want to your property and lord over your family in any way. They don't decide it's lobster and steak every night on you.

If a person with a Resident Visa plays by the rules, more than likely, they will be able to stay much longer than a single year. They can stay for life. But, if they do not behave well, the master of the house will send them off into the darkness and not permit a renewal. Yes, that means deportation with our best wishes and either no stipend or an appropriate allocation.

Chapter 15 A Perfect Plan to Solve a Big Problem

Perfection is tough to achieve

"In order to form a more perfect union...," starts the Preamble of the US Constitution. What does this mean? Well, the Constitution followed the Articles of Confederation which was an agreement among the thirteen colonies to work together but the government as formed was imperfect. So, in the preamble the founders admitted they had tried other forms of creating the union of states but this time, they wanted it to be "more perfect." Than any previous attempt.

Many probably know that over the last ten years, I wrote seven other books dealing with the topic of illegal immigration and the resultant problem of having millions of interlopers as residents in the United States. The book titles are as follows:

- ✓ Taxation Without Representation
- ✓ Americans Need Not Apply
- ✓ No Amnesty! No Way!
- ✓ The Lifetime Guest Plan
- ✓ The Annual Guest Plan
- ✓ 60 Million Illegal Aliens in America!!!
- ✓ Pay-to-Go

This book is my eighth try at building a more perfect plan to deal with what today adds up to just about 60,000,000 uninvited visitors. Each time, as I wrote the next book, I took my improved ideas and I created a better solution but it was not quite perfect. This time, with the Resident Visa Program, it is my best effort yet. I am sure it is not perfect but it is more perfect than anything else that anybody else is proposing.

Though our immigration laws have been strong for a long time, it is obvious that our lax immigration enforcement over the last eight years created confusion as to the real meaning of our laws. It also brought us the problem of people living in the shadows, and this problem is now festering.

One of the big problems in coming up with an acceptable solution is that political ideologies continue to clash over what is fair and right and acceptable. Some want outright legalization and citizenship while others want the letter of the law followed including mass deportations. The laws on the books are simply being ignored by public officials.

President Obama will be remembered as the biggest immigration lawbreaker of all-time. President Trump seems to be listening to what is needed somewhat but he too has put no solution on the table for the 60 million interlopers already residing in our cities. Building a wall is a great idea and it should be done but that is not going to solve the problem of having 60 million illegal residents costing taxpayers from $500 billion to $1 trillion per year.

The 60,000,000 solution

Over time, I kept researching and thinking and researching and thinking and finally it came to me. What if we made a deal with the interlopers and the American people that worked well for both? What if both constituencies, Americans and interlopers could agree to a real solution and be OK with it!

Of course, our politicians would have to be convinced. After reading this book, you will be prepared to understand this is the solution and hopefully, you will do your part to help in the effort to make this plan into a reality. Call your Congressman and Senators.

I have already introduced the Pay-to-Go and the Resident Visa Program. There is a lot of goodness in both of these plans that makes Americans very pleased. The plans are good for Americans and they are also a fair deal and in fact, a good deal for interlopers. These plans should become part of the law of the land quickly. Then, the problem with 60,000,000 shadow aliens in America is solved. Can you imagine. No more shadows? No more of a lot of bad things!

As long as the Resident Visa Holder is well behaved, and we Americans get to define what that means, they will have a right to live in America and hold a job for which an American citizen is not competing. They may keep the jobs they already have.

Resident Visa Holders will be 100% out of the shadows and will live like you and me within our neighborhoods, paying for housing and paying local taxes as we do. Their kids will go to school and they will also pay school taxes like you and me.

In order to be approved for their status of Resident Visa Holder, they first obtain a special resident passport. They must promise not to be a burden (defined as costing taxpayers) or they will be asked to voluntarily return home. The government will help in their return home and in fact will offer substantial assistance of twenty thousand dollars or so for those who agree to go and not come back.

It will not cost American taxpayers a dime for Resident Visa Holders for social services such as education, healthcare or general living. The plan includes no free lunch, aka, no charity. Iron clad identification databases and ID cards with biometrics will be issued and those without such identification will be deported immediately once the program is in full force. With such a generous program available, there should be no reason why interlopers would continue in the shadows.

By law, EMTALA emergency care must be provided to all residents, but these services are not intended to be free. A Resident Visa Holder who receives such benefits can make arrangements through the Accountability system (discussed in later chapters) to pay the fee for their services back to the US Treasury over an extended period if need be. They must not cost taxpayers a dime.

After an interloper in illegal alien status gains a passport from the Post Office or through any other acceptable government agency, they may then apply for their Resident Visa. The normal fee applies for a passport and for a visa as it always has for other visas. The Resident Visa fees will be the same or very similar to other visas. Any additional costs in this process other than the listed fees will also be borne by the interloper. The days of the free-lunch on American taxpayers are gone.

When the plan is in full force, it will include an Accountability System with a record for each interloper. This will establish a record and keep track of financial transactions paid for by the US government, and it will keep a running balance of how much each interloper owes America for the services they have taken from American Taxpayers. No cash payments shall be made although there may be reasons why a limited loan program might be instituted.

The amount to pay back for an interloper will include welfare and healthcare costs from over the years and anything else deemed by officials needing to be repaid. The amount will be determined in the vetting interviews.

In addition to this accounting, those who cannot immediately pay fines and certain fees can have them added to their "account." Resident Visa Holders who work out a deal with officials to not be deported, will be expected to pay a small percentage of this account each year based on need, before their annual visa will be renewed.

A record of the stipends given to those participating in the Pay-to-Go Program will also be accounted. Nothing provided to former interlopers is free. Everything is either paid immediately by the interloper or it is charged to the Accountability system in which reasonable payments will be expected.

To net it out, once the legislation is passed, Resident Visa Holders can begin their freedom in the US tomorrow by getting a special passport at the usual cost. The one-time interloper will temporarily be deemed legal and will not be deported. Most Americans get their passports today at one of many Post Offices in the country and this passport procedure will either be the same or very similar. After the passport, the next step is the Resident Visa application.

When all illegal interlopers have their passports, US officials will know and will have records describing all of the former illegal foreign national residents in the country. Nobody will be hidden. This will have major value to our overall immigration enforcement efforts. At that point, an aspirant for the Resident Visa will become legal. They then must apply for the Resident Visa and be approved or agree to return home if they are not approved.

Those illegal interlopers who choose not to get a Resident Visa have the option of signing up for the Pay-to-Go Return Program and will receive their return home expenses including transportation to their home country as well as a nice stipend by volunteering to return home through the program. They will not be permitted to return to the US.

Americans believe the influx of illegal foreign nationals hurts them and from my own observations, we Americans are 100% correct. The table is turned in this program with American citizens now holding all the TRUMP cards.

To gain their Resident Visa status, interlopers would have to agree to all the stipulations of the program such as to not vote in any election in the US for any office -- local, municipality, state, or federal. Unless they return to their home country, and begin a process like all others from that country, they would never be able to become a citizen of the US.

Jumping the line would not be permitted. However, if their home country, through its normal procedures in conjunction with the US Consular Office agrees to list them on their list for American Citizenship, after making the trip home, they will be able to return to the US using their Resident Visa.

There is no registration per se for the program. The program lasts for a year and is renewable each year thereafter. An illegal interloper would have just one year to acquire their specially designated passport. The passport costs the same as one for Americans traveling abroad. Once they have the passport, they are legal and they would be expected to apply for their Resident Visa within three months.

Most US non-immigration or worker visas have a short time scope, such as three to six months. The Resident Visa, however is designed to be one year in duration. Unlike other visas, it will be renewable annually. For the first five years of the program, the renewal will be in person and will cost $100.00 or the typical cost for a visa, depending on what the government suggests.

Every five years, the Resident Visa Holder would be required to have their photo refreshed just as those re-applying for driver's licenses.

This Resident Visa is not to be thought of as a Guest Worker Visa, such as H-1B, as the recipient is not expected to be hired for any type of work under the auspices of the program. The key point here is that just like worker visas, the Resident Visa Holders are not citizens and they are not permanent residents and they have none of the rights which accrues to citizens.

They not only can hold jobs, they must have a job in order to stay in good status. They are temporary visitors whose Visa type enables them to apply for renewal of their right of residence for one year at a time. As residents only, they have no other rights such as those of today's green-card holder or US Citizen.

In essence, the Resident Visa provides these folks with an opportunity to be treated as visitors of America. They are not American Citizens or ¼ citizens, or ½ citizens and they have none of the rights of citizens.

They are simply temporary visitors and should not expect special treatment. Once approved, they have a special right granted by the citizens of the US to remain in the US as long as they are up-to-date on their Visa renewals and accountability repayments. Plus, of course, they must be well-behaved.

Resident Visa Holders will have no special privileges. American Citizens have all the privileges of citizens in their own country / state, including first-option employment.

There are other advanced notions in the plan that may help US officials deal better with the ongoing issue of people wanting to crash into America uninvited for various purposes.

For example, The Resident Visa Program should never cost the US more than if the plan were not in force. Illegal foreign nationals who are granted a Resident Visa are not permitted to ever become a burden, financial or otherwise upon the citizenry of the USA.

In prior chapters, you read an introduction to a very inclusive plan intended for the benefit of Americans. This Chapter adds detail to the description. Subsequent chapters fine tune the program even further. Though the plan benefits Americans for sure, nonetheless it accommodates over 60,000,000 illegal foreign interlopers, simply because America is a kind nation, and Americans have big hearts.

There is no reason for Americans to pay for visitors, wanted, or unwanted. The tax burden for such interlopers has been very large for taxpayers for many years. The free lunch is over for all but those who choose to take a nice handout and return home from America and not return.

This is a much better deal than the Gang of 8

You may be aware that a group of Senators in 2013 created a monstrous anti-American solution to the same problem solved by the Resident Visa. They did not have the notion of Pay-to-Go in any part of their plan.

I took a hard look at this plan known as the Gang of Eight plan. I also looked at existing law, and other notions about how to solve the nation's problem with illegal residents. I found that none addressed all of the issues that having 60 million illegal foreign nationals in residence brought to America.

When I read the Gang of Eight plan (Rubio, Schumer, Flake, and McCain) in 2013, it was easy to notice that it looked a lot like it was purposely designed to kill America. It did not solve the problem at hand.

With the Gang of Eight plan, no jobs would have been left for Americans; newly unemployed Americans would have to pay for newly minted citizens. Voting in national elections seemed OK for the Gang of 8, as it was not ruled out; 33 million more foreign nationals would be invited. The deal would cost over $6 trillion.

It was a terrible deal for the country. I looked at all of the things that Americans did not like and then looked at what the illegal interlopers liked about living in America. I figured out a way to permit well-behaved interlopers to stay in America with those wanting to go home to take a huge stipend (Pay-to-Go). Having interlopers tucked aside and out of the shadows, would give Americans priority in all ways.

These plans that we have been discussing—Pay-to Go and Resident Visa Plan will work well and will solve the problem while taking a huge financial burden off the backs of Americans.

Now, we all need to make sure Congress gets this done.

Chapter 16 Gang of Eight Compared to Resident Visa Plan

Gang of Eight not as citizen friendly as Resident Visa

We have already discussed the Pay-to-Go Program and the Resident Visa Program in enough detail for understanding its basic precepts and benefits. In this chapter, we compare this innovative notion with the Senate's Gang of Eight fiasco, which Marco Rubio and company tried to ram down our throats in 2013.

So that you know who the treasonous eight scoundrels are who sold all Americans down the river, here is the list. Note there are four Democrats and four RINOS. Eventually, good Americans have to remove these RINOS and all Democrats from the US Senate. They sure do not think like we do.:

- Sen. Michael Bennet, D-CO
- Sen. Richard J. Durbin, D-IL
- Sen. Jeff Flake, R-AZ
- Sen. Lindsey Graham, R-SC
- Sen. John McCain, R-AZ
- Sen. Bob Menendez, D-NJ
- Sen. Marco Rubio, R-FL
- Sen. Chuck Schumer, D-NY

Remember those names. All eight of them are scoundrels. You may recall that in 2013, many of us learned about the Gang of Eight Senators' plan for immigration amnesty for all interlopers. It would have made the Resident Visa Program theoretically unnecessary but it would have gotten us into a deeper mess than we already were in.

Those Americans who think—were not pleased. Low Information Voters accepted it immediately as a good thing. The Marco Rubio Plan was extremely generous to interlopers and very costly to US taxpayers. It was not a fair deal for citizens of the US. Even Rubio's bank account could not have covered all the added expense.

You are going to love the Pay-to-Go Program and the Resident Visa Program. These are 100% America-firs solutions to the problem of having 60 million illegal interlopers living in the shadows. That is a lot of shadows. I'd like to take these folks out of the shadows and do something that will both help them and help Americans.

Why would the liberals—Democrats and Republicans in the US Senate do something like this Gang of Eight perpetration? First of all, it is not an accident. It is exactly what they wanted. It still is what they want. It was not forced upon them. Secondly, I am convinced that these rich Senators in the House of Lords are so removed from the people at large, they are out of touch and have no idea what is happening in the country.

All Senators should be fired, especially those who do not support our new President Donald J. Trump. When Obama had yet to be replaced, I suggested both houses of Congress should be sent home until further notice. They could not or would not put forth good immigration legislation on behalf of the people, claiming Obama would veto it. Well, Obama is gone. Long live President Donald J. Trump.

We all know that more than any other nation in history, the United States has welcomed immigrants in search of a better life. That is why so many citizens got here over the many years from our founding—and even before—while the colonies were being settled.

For their own reasons, the millions of people who regularly enter the US illegally intentionally choose to violate the core principle of the rule of law in the US, and in fact, they mock and belittle the legal naturalization process. They, as illegal interlopers make demands of our kind and generous host country as if they have an entitlement to free services.

You may recall that on September 18, 2017, DACA protesters shouted down one of their own, Nancy Pelosi who had agreed to meet with them. Pelosi was obviously shaken up by the crude interruptions and unruly behavior when ironically, she was on the protesters' side. DACA-supporting protesters stole the show from Pelosi, who tried multiple times unsuccessfully to restore order but instead had to exit through a rear door for her safety when she was outshouted by the crowd.

Pelosi was patient for about 30 minutes during a ceaseless protest. It was no use. She walked out the back door of the building, followed by Reps. Barbara Lee, D-Oakland, and Jared Huffman, D-San Rafael, who were also at the event.

Tucker Carlson of Fox had more compassion for Nancy Pelosi than the DACA recipients and illegal aliens, who were a part of a group of protesters. They were demanding more than Pelosi and the others were willing to give.

Carlson hit the nail on the head in terms of the ingrates in the illegal alien community. They were most disrespectful to a person who has given them just about everything they ever could have asked for. Carlson said DACA protesters showed a "lack of gratitude" for Pelosi and the United States taxpayer, and said that they have no right to demand anything. Carlson made sense. He said that if this situation was occurring in any other country, the citizenry and government would tell the illegal immigrant to "hit the road."

Illegal aliens come to America and want more rights than the citizens of the country. Americans are fed up with it. Pelosi was fed up with it after just thirty minutes. Nonetheless, a continued large-scale influx of new people arrives, without any plan for effective assimilation. In other words, the interlopers want America's benefits but they do not want to adapt in any way to America's culture. Being a good American does not seem to be part of the illegal culture.

It is not just the illegals. I found it difficult to believe that only 40% of green card holders (with permanent resident visas), make the transition to citizenship. They find it comfortable just to stay in the country, collect benefits, and give back nothing. This has occurred over the last 30 years. Today's permanent legal foreign nationals never swear allegiance to America.

As part of the recommendations, once the Resident Visa is adopted, there is little need to continue a green card program in which such a high percentage of permanent residents choose not to make the final step to citizenship. Many others would love the opportunity. Once current green cards expire. The permanent resident should get off welfare and apply for a Resident Visa if they merely want to stay in America.

For their own reasons, too many in green card status do not really want to become Americans. They do want to be treated as Americans for benefits and all good things with all due rights, but they are happy holding allegiance to their home countries. The American people are fed up with this, almost as much as we are fed up with illegal interlopers who are on the American dole.

America, once a melting pot!

America long ago became known as the melting pot for people wanting a new place to live and raise a family. In the early days, immigrants left behind their old ways and they became Americans by choice; and they were proud to become Americans. As they say, they melted in. The identity of the pot from which they emerged said: "AMERICAN."

My father was born 102 years ago in 1915 in America, from a pair of Irish immigrants. He loved America and taught me to love this country. As an example, he would get upset if and when I wore an Irish Sweatshirt. He felt I was bragging about being Irish. He cautioned me, his middle son, that I was an American, not an Irishman. Today's illegal interlopers and many green card holders choose not to identify with America. Yet, in many cases, we provide for their every need.

Unfortunately, for Americans, many interlopers and foreign nationals carry resentment and disdain for our country once they get here. Their negative feelings are exacerbated by an unkind Marxist-leaning media that would rather be typing up the news in Soviet Russia than in America.

We know the truth by its absence in what is called the main stream media. Today they openly love communism as reflected by their reporting. It is obvious that no matter how many communist hammers & sickles or images of Marx, Mao, and other communists the violent Antifa radicals display in their protests in America, , the Fake News media continue to present them as idealistic "anti-fascists." When in fact, they are fascists. Many Americans fall for it and do not believe their own eyes and ears, but they do believe the gospel as preached by the corrupt media.

Only today because of their disgusting narrative to discredit President Trump, do the Democrats claim they no longer like the Russians. I believe nothing the media says. I am a Democrat by Party but today's Democrats have no idea who they really are. They surely do not represent main stream America. And, I am beginning to believe that Democratic leaders would not recognize the truth if they tripped over it.

All of these negatives threaten social cohesion and America's civic culture and our sense of common identity. We are not a diverse country. We are a country of diverse peoples with a common purpose and union. E Pluribus Unum. An especially annoying aspect of today's distortion of immigration is that when immigrants, in legal or illegal status are assimilated into the welfare state rather than into a society of opportunity.

President Teddy Roosevelt gave a speech, that is much needed for today, in 1915. In his speech, he provided this admonition: "The one absolutely certain way of bringing this nation to ruin would be to permit it to become a tangle of squabbling nationalities … A hyphenated American is not an American at all."

We are Americans, not a motley crew of diverse entities with no purpose or no national identity. Remembering we are Americans today is very important regardless of what you might hear from the corrupt media or your friendly crooked politician.

Meaningful reform v charade of eight.

2016 was another bloodbath, as conservatives and nationalists-those who believe in America-first, showed how fed up they were with those who have been shown to be RINOS. They demanded change by voting their minds, and they got it.

Democrat voters always have moved the country further left to Marxism than most Americans in both parties, think is good. In the 2016 general election, even Democrats and most Conservatives and Nationalists decided that enough is enough. President Donald Trump kicked butt as he was the only Republican that the people (Democrats and Republicans) trusted to execute a pro-America strategy rather than go for a Marxist progressive approach.

Gang of Eight Charade

Instead of offering a meaningful reform, such as a real US immigration fix, which would have included Pay-to-Go and a Resident Visa, the corrupt Gang of Eight Senators offered and passed a charade in 2013. Their Bill did not address the intricacies of America's immigration challenges. Instead the Senators offered a magic wand approach to Marxism, hoping to add to the misery of Americans and the poor interlopers caught in the middle.

They pretended that they were solving everything in one colossal bill, with the Democratic Party 100% behind their outlandish overture. Democrats were all ready to take undeserved bows. Yet the Democrats, my party, chose not to do a thing to help regular Americans.

If I convince you that the Bill was bad, please know that it was actually worse than bad. This Bill, S. 744, would have granted immediate amnesty to the estimated 11 million illegal aliens (40 million to 60 million in my estimates) in the country and it "promised" that in the "future," the border would be made secure. Promises when dealing with big liars, are never fulfilled.

You may remember the Secure Fence Act, another lie that was passed 283–138 on September 14, 2006 in the House and on September 29, 2006 in the US Senate. President Bush signed the Secure Fence Act, requiring 700 additional miles of double chain-link and barbed-wire fences with lights and camera poles. But Republican Sen. Kay Bailey Hutchison, authored an amendment that DHS would not be required "to install fencing." The Democrat-controlled Congress passed it. In eleven years just 30 miles of the fence has been built. Congress lies and then deceives the American people.

The Gang of Eight Bill also granted broad new powers to the scandal-ridden Obama Administration and its tab to taxpayers was estimated at $6.3 trillion. Who's got that kind of money? To me, million as a number still is big and billion is 1000 times bigger. Trillion is 1000 times bigger than a billion.

1,000,000,000,000,000

Americans said "no" as quickly as the G-of-8 Bill was passed in the US Senate. Yet, the Senators chose not to listen to the country. Instead they decided to convince us they were right. They fired off paid ads in the form of propaganda in attempts to sell the Bill to the people as something good for Americans, while the House leadership were still debating the legislation.

Americans wholeheartedly rejected it and the House unexpectedly held its ground. In the fall of 2014 the people went ahead and rejected many of the Bill's proponents and sent them packing. Marco Rubio survived to run for President but his betrayal is forever imprinted on the frontal lobes of conservatives and nationalists.

Congress now works for Congress; not the people

The Senate Bill imposed $trillions of additional exorbitant costs on the people, and it was filled with political trade-offs and misguided policies. It offered a continuation of benefits (freebies) to all immigrants; participation in social security; no priority of jobs for Americans; a path to voting and citizenship; and a number of other unsavory aspects. It was as if it were written by a foreign power hoping to overthrow the USA from within.

It seemed to many that the US government was trying to bribe the unwelcome interlopers into accepting a sweet deal that with enough chicanery would be welcomed by an ignorant majority of Americans. Americans, however, woke up, and rose to the front of the opposition and proved in this instance that we are not dumb!

And, so, this Gang of Eight Bill was rejected and with good cause. Beware however, as Americans, that our Senators are not on our side in this battle. We must call them to task on their actions on immigration. They are not free agents. They are supposed to be representatives of the people of the US, accountable to us and not beholden to foreign entities.

Initiative, Referendum, Recall, & Impeachment

With a Republican Congress in 2017, that does not support the President, it is clear that the people need some additional tools of democracy in order to assure that legislators do what is expected. Already, Republicans have balked at the border wall, infrastructure, the budget, and the Obamacare repeal.

It sure would be nice if we the people could use Initiative, Referendum, and Recall at the National level to assure that the will of the people was the mission of our representatives. These tools would make it so that If they did not execute the peoples' will, we could create our own legislation, put petitions on ballots, and in fact we could recall their sorry selves back home and put them out of office without having to wait for elections.

Few conservatives would not agree that Democratic leadership in the last twenty years at the federal level has morphed into the Marxist Party. In this Party remake, individual initiative and survival of the fittest no longer matter.

At the municipal level, the people, Democrats and Republicans have not adopted this hard-left Marxist philosophy and simply want our representatives to be trustworthy and do what is right for us.

In fact, unfortunately for the health of America, most people do not pay enough attention to government. However, never before in our history since the revolution has vigilance to the actions of public servants ever been more necessary. Politicians of today will take your wallet from your front pocket, stare you in the face, and blame the guy next to you.

Then, they will try to talk you into believing that you did not see what you clearly observed. They will put it on the News as news, though it is fake. There is little value for honesty or the truth in today's Democrat Party.

We get the government we deserve

We get the government we deserve. It is not the people; it is our leaders who have betrayed us on issue after issue. But, it is we the people who must hold the leaders accountable. We must pay attention. The founders told us that is our job. We are too trusting.

We should not be asking politicians for special favors for it emboldens them. If we send them home for good, they cannot hurt us again.

The Marxist-leaning Democratic leadership of today would reject JFK if he appeared as a candidate against Hillary Clinton, the "lady" who was heir apparent in the Democrat Party to replace President Obama. I thank God that it is Donald Trump who took over peaceably on January 20.

In the beginning of this chapter, I promised we would look at Pay-to-Go Program and the Resident Visa Program and see how it compares to the traitorous Gang of Eight Senate-endorsed program. In the below section, and in the accompanying chart, we can see the utter guano that Marco Rubio and the Gang of Eight tried to force feed Americans.

I contrast Chuck Schumer, John McCain, and Rubio's Gang of Eight Bill with the Pay-to-Go and the Resident Visa Plans. It shows that certain Senators have a different agenda than we do. When their time comes to be reelected, I hope their states cast them out.

In our cursory analysis so far, you may not have been sure that the Pay-to-Go and the Resident Visa were a good deal for you. So, this comparison / summation is designed to open your eyes. if you were ambivalent on the sincerity of the Gang of Eight plan before, these facts should convince you that there was a sellout of Americans in play in 2013, spearheaded by the US Senate. A stodgy group of tired old farts, who no longer care about America, have turned against the people. John McCain has a leadership position among these traitors.

Thankfully, Americans stopped them this time, and we stopped the Democrats and Hillary Clinton in November 2916. They were prepared to give us more unlawful, unchecked migrations and unvetted refugees—but we the people picked Donald Trump instead.

Fortunately, forever, President Obama, the one-time Energizer Bunny, who refused to die many times from the first-time Sarah Palin finished him off in the VP debate, will no longer be around to reject the will of the people by breaking the Constitution. Obama's goal had been to provide the interlopers the freebies they wanted without asking for congressional approval. When he was president, he did little for America and Americans.

This lawless behavior brought about the beginning of the ruination of our country. Since the 2016 elections, many loyal Americans are counting our new blessings. I think many of us if invited would have attended the past President's farewell party. After all, we were hoping we could have made it happen four years sooner.

So that we know where we would be if Mrs. Clinton, and the Gang of Eight, including wimpy Republicans like John McCain, Jeff Flake, Lyndsey Graham, and Marco Rubio, had their way, we now compare the Pay-to-Go Program and the Resident Visa (Resident Visa) Program with the Guano Plan of the G-of-8. It is absolutely a necessary step. We cannot forget who sold us out.

The Gang of Eight didn't play it straight

Americans throughout 2013 heard the constant drumbeat about the Gang of Eight's Amnesty program. Before we wrap up this book with more reasons for the Pay-to-Go and the Resident Visa, let's compare bullet by bullet, the Gang of Eight plan (G of 8) with the Resident Visa plan. The bullets are self-explanatory. This may be a real eye-opener for some—especially those who think Rubio and company are on our side.

2013 Gang of Eight v Resident Visa

	G of 8	Resident Visa
Border secure	No	Yes
Jobs	Favors Interloper	Favors Americans
Amnesty	Yes	No
Path to citizenship	Yes	No (almost same as today)
Permanent residents	Yes	Never, renewable visa
Voting	Yes	No, Never
Welfare benefits	Yes	No, Never
Freebies	Yes	No, Never
Anchor babies	Yes	No, stipends to depart
Employer fees/fines	No	Yes -if one employee
Reunification	33M in 10yrs	Not for Resident Visa Holders
Coerced-deportation	None	As needed for violations
Self-return to home	No	Pay nice stipend
Must have healthcare	No	Yes
Must be employed	No	Yes
Must speak English in 2 yrs?	No	Yes
Oath of allegiance	No	Yes, after 1 year
Cost/debt accountability	No	Yes
Taxpayer Costs	$ 6Trillion	Zero
Payback plan	No	Yes
Accountability Database	No	Yes
Interloper fine	Yes	Yes
Employer fine	No	Yes (help finance program)
Back taxes	No	Yes (interview)

Chapter 17 Review of the Resident Visa Program

How does the Resident Visa Plan actually work?

The one undeniable aspect of the Resident Visa plan is that it would relieve the US taxpayer of a huge, unsustainable annual cost burden. The raw cost of services at all government levels to support illegal aliens is approaching $500 Billion per year. But, the American taxpayer pays more than just their share of the cost. It affects their income also.

The National Academy of Sciences found that, on average, immigration causes the wages of competing American workers to go down by 5.2 percent. Immigration redistributes approximately $500 Billion in wages from American workers to employers of low-wage immigrants. It helps businesses but not regular Americans who simply can no longer afford liberal plans to pay the full freight for illegal interlopers. Add all the wage and job losses together and you get the $500 Billion.

When the Resident Visa plan is implemented, all of these costs are gone after just one year. Those who return to the home country cost nothing and those who agree to forego benefits in order to gain the Resident Visa and come out of the shadows will cost nothing. The impact on regular Americans will be about $1 Trillion counting the cost savings and the new job and higher wage opportunities.

When President Trump gets his copy of this book, containing the Pay-to-Go and the Resident Visa Plans, the implementation will not be far off. So, if you ever have the opportunity, please slip the President a copy of this book. I will mail him one but too many people get to filter his mail for me to be sure he will ever get a copy.

When I researched typical passport costs, they cost about $120.00 and when I researched typical Visa costs, the cost is $160.00, Since most visas are not annually renewable as is the Resident Visa, I would expect the cost of an annual renewal of a Resident Visa would be between $100.00 and $200.00 depending on what it costs the government to implement. Since this is not a full proposal for a Congressional Bill, there are no guarantees on what other levies Congress would place within their legislation.

The Pay-to-Go and the Resident Visa Plans are both process driven. Nothing is by chance. The Resident Visa process begins as you would expect. All 60 million illegal interlopers would be given six months to get a passport. By getting their special passport, they would have in essence signed up (registered) as an illegal alien with the United States Government. At this point, they are legal, and there are no more shadows. Their next step is that they must apply for the Resident Visa.

Once the six month period for gaining passports is over, all interlopers by US decree will have a changed status and the status quo will have changed. Either the former illegal aliens will have gained legal passports or the illegal aliens would continue to be illegal aliens because they chose to take no action regarding their passport. If they do not take our generous offer, they would become the #1 targets of coerced deportation from the United States or of course, they could sign up for Pay-to-Go.

The first step in the Resident Visa process for an illegal alien is not very complicated. An illegal alien must first get a special resident passport within six months at various government sites, typically post offices, across the country. This process collects necessary information from the applicant and typically results in the granting of the passport, which is delivered in the mail. Nothing in the passport process, however, happens overnight.

Once a former illegal alien gains their special passport, they are enabled to apply for a Return Home Stipend or a Resident Visa.

The Pay-to-Go Program is fairly straight forward as the candidate simply brings forth their passport and signs up for the particular stipend for which they are entitled and their departure is scheduled. They get a free ticket to their home country, some pocket change, and a voucher for a big fat stipend. The stipend will be delivered to them by a bank in their home country.

The Resident Visa Program will require two types of personal interviews. One will assure demographic data is complete and the other will assess the fees, fines, and any debt payback for years of collecting welfare using fake-id's. When approved, the Resident Visa will be granted, the computer records will be created, and the visa holder will receive their ID card.

I see three potential types of beneficiaries who may participate in both the Pay-to-Go and the Resident Visa Programs. In Pay-to-Go, of course, the individual at US taxpayer expense will be provided with the customary travel fares and dinners / lunches that are appropriate and scheduled by the US Customs Office. In other words, the departee will pay nothing out of pocket to arrive in his / her home country. Additionally, a stipend voucher will be given.

Th program is designed for the 60 million illegal interlopers residing in the country. However, the Pay-to-Go Program can save the US another ton of funds if it is also used to attract green card holders on welfare, and anchor babies on welfare.

The green card holders and anchor citizens can choose to stay in their current status or sign up for a Resident Visa or Pay-to-Go. So, they can stay in America or return to their home countries with stipends. There would no longer be a cost of their welfare for the US.

The three categories are as follows:

1. Current interlopers
2. Legal green card holders on welfare
3. Anchor babies at any age, including children supervised by a legal or illegal parent.

The recommended stipend for each of the three categories is as follows:

1. Current Interlopers	$20,000
2. Legal Green Card Holders on Welfare	$30,000
3. Anchor Babies or Adults	$50,000

Anybody opting for a stipend for Pay-to-Go in any of the above categories would be prohibited without special petition from every returning to the United States for any reason. Any debt accrued that is accounted for in the Accountability system (next chapter) would be collected prior to any request for readmission to be examined.

Other uses for this program to make a point

No new system should be designed with just one objective when there are so many clearly similar objectives known at the time of design. For example, I see five distinct sets of people data and a catch-all that should be part of the same system design. They are as follows:

1. 60 million illegal interlopers who are in country today
2. Illegal visa over stayers
3. Legal visa holders
4. Green card holders and other legal residents
5. Anchor babies even if over 21 yrs. of age
6. Other foreigners in the US

I place other at the bottom of the list as a catch-all. I am sure that there are some off the wall cases of foreigners such as diplomats etc. that do not demand a separate system.

The 60 million interlopers

Before I continue, may I remind you again that my concern in this book is not border security; it is not E-verify; it is not the visa system; and it is not green card holders or anchor citizens. My objective is to come up with a system design that is durable and I have done that. It solves the problem of the 60 million illegal interlopers in this country today. It happens that the design can be used to help the US better handle green card holders and birthright citizens if they ever become a priority.

We are a smart enough country that we should have solved this years ago but we obviously have not had officials with a will to do so. This is another reason I thank the Lord for a man so able and willing to pitch in as President Trump.

With a Pay-to-Go Program and a Resident Visa system operational, there may be other opportunities for synergy by creating a base computer system that will solve the problem for all types of permanent resident or temporary resident foreigners or illegal-entry foreigners residing in this country at this time and perhaps times in the future. Let's review the financial impact of the programs.

Suppose there were 5 million interlopers receiving the Pay-to-Go stipend, what would be the numbers? It would cost $100 billion to implement in the first year. That would be 5 million times the $20,000 stipend amount—5M X 20K= $100 Billion as the one-year cost of the stipends. S

Since supporting illegal aliens cost $30,000 per person per year, we multiply this by the 5 million interlopers to get the total cost 5M X 30K =$150 Billion. This would have been the cost but since the 5 million have left the country, this is the savings.

The gross savings is thus $150 Billion. When we subtract the stipend cost for 5 million interlopers returning to the home country. We have a net cost savings of $50 Billion.

In subsequent years, since there would be no cost for the already paid stipends, each year would bring another $250 billion per year in savings for 5 million. Since sixty million is twelve times 5 million and since the estimate is 60 million interlopers. Can you imagine the cost savings if all interlopers took the Pay-to-Go? To get this amount, we multiply 12 X $250Billion = $3 Trillion savings per year.

The stipend would cost the US about $100 billion to implement but it would all come back by not having to pay annual benefits. It would all be reclaimed in the second year of the program and every year thereafter.

The short view of the program is that after gaining the passport Pay-to-Go, the new registrant signs on the dotted line and agrees to abide by the terms of the program, including no lawsuits. The first half of the payment occurs when the interloper reaches the home country and within 6 months of the first payment, he or she collects the second payment to complete the stipend amount.

Accept the Pay-to-Go or Apply for the Resident Visa

The Pay-to-Go plan is very generous in its desire for unhappy illegal interlopers to go back to their home countries and reestablish their lives. As such, after registration, the US will provide a special credit card that can be used only by the interloper and only for authorized travel to their home country. The stipend will be available at the interlopers' bank in the home country.

All interlopers with passports for the Resident Visa, who after vetting are approved and not deemed to be bad guys can sign up and pay the fee for the Resident Visa. This enables them to stay in the US under the terms of the visa. This visa may be renewed annually. As noted, after year 1, an oath of allegiance must be taken to get the first renewal, and after year two, the Resident Visa holder must pass a literacy test and an English test in order to be accepted for renewal for the third year.

Other special conditions may be included by US officials in the event time expires at any stage of the process, and the registrant has neglected the call and has simply chosen not to move forward to complete the process. Those who do not pass either the English test or the literacy test may opt for extensions in order to pass the tests. If they choose not to take the extensions, they would automatically be enrolled in the Pay-to-Go Program. If they fail to arrive in their home country under the program, they will receive no stipend and will be deported in the customary fashion.

Is the Pay-to-Go Program acceptance automatic?

Yes, it is automatic. There is no reason to deny such interlopers their opportunity to go home at this time. So, if they apply, they will be accepted.

Is the Resident Visa program acceptance automatic?

No, it is not automatic. Besides the casual passport interview and data collection, two additional interviews are required. They both may occur at the time of the visit to the official station. The first is a general vetting about worthiness to be part of the program. The second is to determine finances and debts that may be deemed payable to the US under the accountability system.

Even the gang of 8 program had a $2,000 fine imposed for the illegal entry. Whatever fees or fines are determined by officials will be assessed for those qualifying for the Resident Visa during the finance interview. The payments can be made over time using the accountability system so as to not be extremely burdensome. The accountability system is explained in the next chapter.

Two Resident Visa interviews (aka double vetting)

Interlopers, who choose to gain a Resident Visa go through a process that includes obtaining a special passport and they undergo several vetting interviews to prove their worthiness in America and to American citizens. During the interviews, the applicants agree to a number of stipulations that permit them to get out of the shadows permanently and begin to enjoy all benefits of holding a Resident Visa as a temporary visitor of the Unites States of America. The shadows will be eliminated and sanctuary cities will be gone once the Resident Visa is in force.

The interviews will be extensive though much of the information may be collected online at the applicant's choosing and during the passport processing. The precepts of the "deal" are clear. Among all other detailed stipulations, the applicant also agrees to pay an annual renewal fee in addition to whatever fines, fees, & taxes are determined by US officials.

In order to be admitted, the applicant agrees to be "well-behaved." The idea of "well-behaved" is a notion that is to be defined each year by the immigration service of the US. The applicant also agrees to hold a job; to obtain his or her own healthcare insurance; and to never vote while being in Resident Visa status. They also agree that they understand that for new jobs, American citizens have priority always.

Additionally, the applicant promises to take no freebies ever from the US, States, or Municipal Governments. In other words, they agree never to take benefits from the US ever again—especially in healthcare, education, and cash payments.

They agree that they will not ever claim federal child credit to gain unwarranted tax refunds as has been frequently done in the past. Only US citizens can receive benefits from any of the US systems, including the IRS. Most importantly they promise to stay clean and be good residents of America.

In case you may think that tax credit fraud is uncommon and would be chump change if we stopped it, think again. In 2011, your friendly IRS sent more than $46 million in tax refunds to 23,994 "unauthorized" alien workers who all listed the same address in Atlanta, Ga. Can you imagine how widespread this type of fraud actually is. This was uncovered in an audit report by the Treasury Inspector General for Tax Administration (TIGTA).

Those applying for a Pay-to-Go stipend or a Resident Visa, are not obligated to agree to any of the stipulations which are put forth. However, if they decide not to abide by all the stipulations, by way of their applications, by default, they have agreed to self deport with no stipend.

In this full process, there will be fines and fees up front besides the passport and visa fees depending on what government officials feel need to be collected. If such amounts cannot be paid immediately, they may be "charged" to the accountability system. Besides fines, etc. taken on account if the applicant has no resources, the Resident Visa Holder must pay out of pocket an estimated $100.00 to $200.00 renewal fee for each year of approval.

Their financial database record called an Electronic Accountability Record (EAR) and smart card information will be updated with each on-site renewal and major change to demographics. If they abide by the rules and renew their status every year, they can live in the US forever, without fear of deportation. But, they must renew their application in person every year.

Otherwise, they have chosen to ignore our generous hand, and deportation either via the Pay-to-Go Program or via self-deportation is the only option available. It is a simple plan; a simple process; that is fair to all. It solves the problem of as many as 60 million interlopers for good. You have just read about the essence of the program. The Pay-to-Go Program and the Resident Visa plans are such good ideas that they can help in other areas to assure the US gets all the benefits.

Children

Children, must also register for one of the two new programs. They too must get passports and be approved. Anybody 18 years of age or older is considered an adult.

The Pay-to-Go and the Resident Visa programs solve the problem for DACA children also. As a DACA concession, the Resident Visa will be no charge for the first five years. Those in the DACA program also qualify for the Pay-to-Go Program if they do not want to stay in the US.

Summary of benefits:

- No more shadows
- No more freebies
- No more illegal voting
- No more job priority for interlopers
- No more sanctuary cities
- No more path to citizenship without starting at home country
- No more cost to Taxpayer

Pay-to-Go Program and the Resident Visa Plan Summary

In summary, the major points in the SD/RV plan are as follows:

- Addresses all American concerns on America's side
- Resident Visa gives right to reside in America and hold jobs
- No freebies; no voting; no citizenship; jobs for citizens 1st
- All applicants first must obtain special passport
- Then either Pay-to-Go or Resident Visa
- Can tke a stipend and return to home country
- Pay-to Go paid in home country
- All applicants for Pay-to-Go accepted.
- Can choose to obtain a Resident Visa
- Requires 2 vetting interviews; pay fees, fines.
- Interview 1 – demographics; Interview 2 – financial
- All interloper debt kept in Electronic Accountability Record
- Debt collected slowly over time
- Must get special passport in one year
- Must pay any assessed fines, costs, back taxes

Program participants are on temporary visas and are not eligible as benefit recipients

Temporary visas in the US by law provide no benefits for visitors. Foreign visitors to the U.S. must have travel insurance with coverage for emergency medical emergencies and evacuations prior to their trip. This would not change with the new programs. This will affect those interlopers who are using fake-id to receive medical care today. This loophole will be eliminated.

To qualify for the programs, before an applicant signs on the dotted line for their special Pay to Go or Resident Visa passport, they must agree to a number of provisos. By signing, they accept each and every proviso and future added provisos. They cannot pick and choose. They are not citizens and do not have the rights of citizens. Use of fake id will again be a crime in the US. The taxpayers of the US as citizens are the masters. These provisos include the following:

- Fake ID not permitted
- Speak English in 2 years
- English test each renewal
- Participants have no citizenship rights
- A child resident must get a Resident Visa
- Guests may have children in US but must agree their offspring are not anchor citizens. They are automatic Resident Visa Holders.
- Program is at pleasure of Congress & President
- Must renew status once a year.
- Must permit Photo ID & databases to be updated
- Must pay annual fee & something towards debt.
- This is not an amnesty program.
- Debt is accountable and payable via Accountability System (next chapter)
- Debt does not require immediate deportation
- No US family reunification provisions for green cards
- When green cards expired, LPR transfers to Resident Visa. Last chance for citizenship via green card
- US will assist with family reunification in home country
- Special program for former Anchor Babies and former Green Card holders
- Anchor Babies & Green Card Holders qualify for voluntary Pay-to Go & Resident Visa Program can
- Visa holders cannot vote
- Visa holders May keep jobs at minimum wage or more
- For new jobs, American Citizens have preference
- Requires strict enforcement of all current laws
- Obama immigration amnesties repealed
- Other stipulations as defined by Congress and President Trump

Chapter 18 Financial Accountability System

All loans require pay back

When a good friend or relative asks for some money to help her through a crisis, if you are like me, you give her what she needs to the extent you can afford it. After all, you too may be in the same situation in the future. When you do this, do you simply withdraw from your account and add it to hers? Is that the last time you expect to ever see the amount of the help even if she wins the Lottery the next day? Do you have any claim to what you have given her? Do you and she know there is a debt due when her conditions are more positive?

Other than for close family matters, which are often unaccountable, most friends help friends as much as possible financially but the amounts given are expressed or implied loans, and both parties know a payback is expected if things get better. Everybody hopes for the best but a good friend knows that it may take a long time for a payback to occur. In the main, there are no huge gifts from one to another. Yes, eventually loans may be forgiven but by the choice of the lender not the borrower.

There is an old saying that is reflected in the song, *Robinson Crusoe,* sung by Al Jolson. When he described his pal, Friday, to show that he was a good man, in the song, Crusoe noted that "*He did not borrow or lend.*" You remember in Shakespeare's Hamlet, 1602, Polonius said: "*Neither a borrower nor a lender be…*" Borrowing and lending are tricky deals among friends and often result in the friendship disappearing and the kind lender never being paid back. In the big financial institutions, you know as a borrower, you must pay every last penny plus interest.

How is it then, that the government is able to send huge amounts of dollars and in-kind contributions to citizens and even non-citizens for their welfare and support? From the taxpayers through the government, there are many who receive cash payments, rent subsidies, medical payments, etc. Are these gifts?

Would you believe that the government does not keep track of any of this? Why? Good question! The answer is because our government is inept. There is no database anywhere keeping track of anything. Yet, the government has given away untold $Trillions of unaccountable benefits. To whom. How much? When? Why? It is safe to say that nobody in the government knows and worse than that, nobody cares because we the people permit it by reelecting the people who pass such insane laws.

Does government actually give gifts?

Are there government gift-giving provisos in the Constitution? No, there are none. Rugged individualism (and the early Patriots were tough folks) demands individuals take care of their own needs. Are any benefits that anybody receives from government without payment to be thought of as "gifts" from the government? No, that would be unconstitutional as the government is not permitted to take anything from Harry to give to Jack or Josephine.

Who is the government that can't do this yet does it anyway? Are the gifts really from congresspersons as the receiver may believe? Are the gifts from the President as the receiver may believe? Who is it that is giving all these gifts?

Hard as it may be for taxpayers to believe, the gifts received by those selected by government are directly from the taxpayers. Government has no money or assets of its own. Since it is your money and not the government's money, the government has decided to not even bother remembering to whom they gave what. Nobody in the government, after the huge gifts are sent out every week, accounts as to the amount of the gifts, or who received the gifts. They never suggest that the "gifts" are to be paid back because just like real gifts, they do not have to be paid back. There are no *payment for gift* collectors in the US government.

Do any of us think this a good system for America?

And, so suppose just a day after a $2,500 government gift in the form of a check or a direct deposit goes to Joe Dokes, Mr. Dokes also receives notification from the Powerball Lottery that his ship came in for $361,000,000. Would you expect Joe Dokes to choose not to contact the Lottery Commission to gain the payment proceeds? Would anybody expect Dokes to say, "Thanks but no thanks." I think nobody would expect anybody to not take the cash..

Do you think the government that just gave Dokes $2500 the day before would be looking for that money back? Nope! They do not even know Dokes got the $2500. They therefore do not care that Dokes is now rich. In fact, you can bet that nobody in government crosschecks Lottery winners against welfare recipients. Therefore, next month, Dokes more than likely will again be $2500 richer.

Even if a Big Four auditing firm in the course of checking the US Treasury accounts receivable had full access to all the records, they would not find any entry indicating that Joe Dokes owes the government one of many $2,500 repayments. Why? Because it was a gift! At least the government accounts it as a gift, expecting and receiving no repayment.

Now, if we chose to call these amounts helping loans instead of gifts, with no corresponding change in accounting (still no tracking), I would bet a small percentage, but at least a few people nonetheless, would try to pay back the government when extremely better times came about?

Why do we treat them as gifts? The recipient certainly did not earn a gift or a benefit as they have with Social Security, Medicare, or Unemployment, which are more or less contributory. I do not even want to know the answer. I am sure that it is tough enough being a great politician giving one taxpayer gift after another to one voter after another to ever suggest that the indebted voter might actually ever be compelled to repay the gift!

Who gets the gifts?

Who knows? There is no list? If the government does not know to whom they give the gifts or the values of the gifts, then collection or a requested repayment is impossible. We do know that there are over eighty different welfare schemes that give gifts to recipients on a regular basis. All of the "programs" have names and none of them, other than student loans, demand repayment.

The apparent givers of the gifts, the politicians, can never be blamed, since nobody will ever be asking and therefore, nobody will be asked for a loan repayment. The real giver of the gift, the taxpayers effectively have no say or we would be clamoring for accountability. We should be and it would OK if we began to clamor right now!

Welfare and medical services and 79 other US benefits are simply free for the taking, and they are killing US. You bet they are. Not one dime has ever been accounted for or collected on taxpayers' behalf. Yet, we as a country are $20 trillion in debt. Who designed this system? Politicians. It is how they get reelected.

Here are just a few of the 80 + programs:

- ✓ Medicaid
- ✓ EITC and Child Tax Credit
- ✓ SNAP
- ✓ SSI
- ✓ Housing Assistance
- ✓ Pell Grants
- ✓ TANF
- ✓ Child Nutrition
- ✓ Head Start
- ✓ Employment & Training
- ✓ WIC
- ✓ Child Care
- ✓ LIHEAP

Politicians actually believe money grows on trees.

There is no accountability because Congress wants it that way. Congress wants to be duly recognized by the receivers of the largesse as the grand giver. They want people to feel indebted to them, though it is not them, it is you and I, the American taxpayers who fork out the dole received by interlopers and others with no accountability.

They get to buy votes with taxpayer dollars with no repayment required. No government "gift" should be an eternal gift. Government should not be permitted to give "gifts." Find gifts in any articles of the Constitution or the Bill of Rights, or even a mention of gifts from government in the Federalist Papers. You won't! It was not how our country was founded.

Illegal foreign nationals and many others, with no chance or desire of ever making a payback, get gifts from the taxpayers via Congress all the time. It keeps the Treasury department quite busy assuring all the gifts are given on-time. Who is being played for a fool here? When the receiver is an illegal foreign national, they more than likely have been instructed by other illegal foreign interlopers to take the money and run, and don't worry…be happy! They know that the US will have no idea who they are.

The Resident Visa Plan solves this problem for good. We track immigrant / interloper / guest debts. That is why this plan will be hard to get introduced or passed in Congress without Americans getting involved. Of course, the plan would work even if the accountability were taken away so let's not forget that. But, it helps to remember that Congress loves giving away your money!

Cost Accountability

Accountability for Resident Visa Holder debt is a major feature of the Resident Visa Plan. However, it would help all of America if it became a part of all US welfare plans eventually. I am not talking about earned things like Social Security, Medicare, and

Unemployment Compensation. Anything that helps anybody think that not working is the preferred action to assure benefits is on my target list. It should be on your target list also.

And, so with regard to the Resident Visa Plan, any aspirant who becomes a visa holder can stay in the US until asked to leave for some violation of the requirement to be well-behaved. They are on their own financially just like you and I. By law (if passed appropriately) as visitors on a resident visa, they are prohibited from taking from the US welfare system.

When Resident Visa Holders who really try to keep up with their payments to taxpayers—run into issues in repayment, I would recommend that they should not be treated too harshly at first. As soon as they are back on top, they should be required to get back on the payment track as soon as possible.

Their financial transactions leading to debt to the US Treasury, under the plan, would all be captured in what I would call an Electronic Accountability Record (EAR) in the US Accountability database. This database would be proof enough that the days of the free lunch are over. There would be no amnesty. There would be no welfare state just for having been an illegal foreign national with a Resident Visa. If this legislation is enacted, those days are gone. Everything is accounted.

Eventually, former interlopers would have to pay this back or figure out the best way to leave the country.

Keeping an accounting of illegal interloper debt is as great a start for this program and for the United States as is registering and granting passports to the 20 to 60 million interlopers for the first time for the normal $120.00 in fees. Once debt is accounted, it can then be collected, even if it is piecemeal.

Attempts to collect need to be made that are not too harassing to citizens or newly minted Resident Visa holders to assure payment or partial payments on a regular payment plan. Over a proper amount of time, Resident Visa Holders must pay back all accrued debt on their record and any future debt they may be permitted to accrue. Heirs and assigns should be required to pay some portion of an inherited estate to reduce the debt balance of a deceased.

Access to database records

Each record in the Resident Visa database as well as the Accountability database would be accessible via multiple access keys. These would include by ID #, somewhat like a Social Security #; by name; by address; by fingerprints, by retina scan, etc. Of course, the ID should not be a social security number. The Resident Visa and all other access keys would be encoded magnetically in the ID card in the same fashion as card numbers are recorded in charge cards.

A bar code, an RFID chip, fingerprint, retina, and facial scans would also be recorded from the vetting interviews and they would all be be verifiable. They would come into play from the point of the registration (passport) process and the guest photo ID card. Any of these ID features would be able to be used to access data in the Resident Visa or ACCT databases for those with authority to do so.

The data could be fetched therefore via biometrics or a verified ID, name, address, etc. Since a resident visa holder could be identified by a finger print, they could never snooker the US system into thinking they are a dead guy or somebody else whose ID they may have stolen. Drivers licenses in all states should also be encoded with the ID so that its presentation as required in certain authorization schemes would be the same as citizens.

Americans do not want to be messed with!

Reality says that in a US in which most people do not want to deport the poor souls living in the shadows, how do we get the "shadow people" to begin paying US back for what they have taken over the years? First of all, the Resident Visa is optional. It gives a former illegal interloper the legal right to stay in the US. If during the special passport application, an illegal interloper does not agree to pay their fine or any debt as determined by the US Agent doing the vetting, they may self deport, be deported by coercion, or they may sign up for the Pay-to-Go program.

Americans are not happy about the authorized theft of taxpayer dollars in the form of gifts that have been granted over the years by the prior POTUSes and the Congress.

What if we came up with a standard way of paying back US taxpayers for those interlopers who eventually become Resident Visa Holders? What would it look like? What would the standard required payback actually look like? Let's take a shot at building the scenario in simple terms:

The standard payback:

- Must pay 10% of debt or 10% of income each year
- Requirement to renew as a Resident Visa Holder.
- Can gain special repayment waivers for hardships during annual interviews.
- Additional processing cost- waivers added to record
- To repeat: No free lunch!

Let's review some of the jobs notions for the Resident Visa.

Resident Visa favors Americans for jobs!

The list on the following page summarizes the impact of The Resident Visa Plan on Jobs:

- Pre-Resident Visa --Favors Interloper; cheap wages
- Post Resident Visa -- Favors Americans, not mean spirited
- Resident Visa = Jobs much more available for Americans
- Resident Visa = Visa holders may keep current jobs
- Resident Visa = Citizens prioritized v Visa holders for new jobs

Do Americans feel taken?

Americans are not dummies. We just have been lulled over a number of years of good government that such good government would continue. It has not continued. In fact, today's style of government is unacceptable for honest Americans. Who in the US can be pleased with this system of government given to us today by corrupt, arrogant, and greedy politicians?

In the notion of no freebies, as a requirement of the Resident Visa, a corollary, is that every Resident Visa Holder pays for everything. Let's honestly ask ourselves: "If not them, then whom?"

Place yourself in the role of a visa holder, recently freed from the shadow of deportation. If you are a Resident Visa Holder, having once broken into the USA, and now, having broken away from your days as an interloper, should you not be pleased?

If you are not pleased, should you expect that somebody who you have never met will step up and say they will pay all your expenses because you would like to live in America, expense free? Sorry, unless you find such a person, it would be best to appreciative your new freedom. Your expenses are on you, however—nobody else.

Government will not pay for you once you get your Resident Visa. It may be tough to reconcile but the new plan says that any financial burden incurred by you will not be paid by US taxpayers—even if we once paid for those with fake ID's in the past, when many more people were in the shadows.

Sunshine with no shadows

Celebrate the Sun. The Resident Visa Plan is a sunshine plan. Enjoy your tan. There are no shadows. Everything is in the open. Just do not ask American taxpayers to pay anything for your sustenance.

Charitable organizations such as the Salvation Army, Catholic Social Services, Jewish Charities of America, National Association of Free and Charitable Clinics. Shriners and St. Jude's Hospital to name a few, as well as many others are ready to help Americans or Resident Visa Holders who need help with all types of issues. Government will not make payments to Resident Visa Holders under the Resident Visa. Period!

Here is a list of a few important notions that will help make this plan work for interloper and American taxpayer alike

- Visa Holders live and work freely in the US
- Visa Holders must be employed
- Visa Holders must have healthcare
- Citizens will no longer pay for EMTALA
    - Emergency Medical Treatment & Active Labor Act
- Resident Visa may use EMTALA as all US citizens but must pay for it, when billed, just as a citizen.
- EMTALA and all such emergency debt may be added to the visa holder's accountability record
- Obamacare or its replacement w/o subsidies must be made available for resident visa holders to purchase… no freebies and no subsidies.
- Jobs for Americans first; Visa holders may keep current jobs; No voting ever with a visa, No welfare.

The accountability database will contain an Electronic Accountability Record (EAR), similar to an Electronic Health Record (EHR), or an Electronic Medical Record (EMR). This is a unique idea for a government that likes to give one person's dollars to another without ever keeping track of how much was given to whom. Today, regardless of the service, there is never a request for a payback of taxpayer dollars. This changes with the Resident Visa Program. Accountability will be foremost and built into the program.

Payback

Politicians like to gain favor by spending Mary's dollars to give five different Joe's a break. They buy votes with all of our dollars. They rarely have sympathy for those they help. They hold them accountable for no payback—just a lifelong silent commitment to keep the villain politicians in office for having provided the favors. Even Mary and Joe who benefit, think the system is corrupt.

This corrupt system kills us domestically as it is the norm in our welfare system and it is killing us on the immigration front. It not only costs taxpayers as much as $500 billion per year, it serves as a huge magnet for the world to ignore our borders, and simply "come on down!"

Once the incentive for freebies is gone, only the productive members of any other society will try to come to America. The quality of our new citizens and our guests will increase. If they do not like America, their applications for residence or Resident Visa status will be rejected because we do not like people who do not like our country.

Valid in Health Information Technology Systems Also!

Today in the Health Information Technology realm, computerized database systems already can accommodate Electronic Medical Records (EMRs) and Electronic Health Records (EHRs). Even in the domestic health industry with so many payments coming from government in the form of welfare for health purposes and EMTALA, I would propose a new record type called the Electronic Accountability Record (EAR). But that is not the focus of this book. I have mentioned it multiple times as the Resident Visa cannot exist well for very long without an EAR system.

Let's define the three databases which we have been lightly discussing since we began this book adventure. Two are currently used in all Health Management Software in doctors' offices and in hospitals, clinics and pharmacies. The third is being proposed in this book to accommodate those Resident Visa Holders who simply cannot pay off a huge debt in a short period of time.

- EMR Electronic Medical Record – Doctors or health services provider's local database patient record

- EHR Electronic Health Record – Doctors or providers sharable database patient record kept in a national database [in the sky!]

- EAR Electronic Accountability Record—Doctors or providers' sharable database and / or an immigration database of financial data used to capture and store all paid and unpaid charges & payments [in the sky!]

There would be an EAR record today if the Resident Visa were implemented. Its data would be housed within the Accountability database which would be in synch with the Resident Visa Holder Program.

The US medical system has no such financial database because everything is free if it is sponsored by government. That means it is paid by taxpayers who have no say.

Should there be accountability to the taxpayers?

Before we modify the US Visa Systems to accommodate a financial accountability system for Resident Visa Holders, rather than deport everybody who owes the US a dime, and never collect anything, we need a system. We must have a way to assure that we can capture the amounts due to the US Treasury or other government treasuries such as those in states, counties, and municipalities. Why should the services provided to any illegal foreign national not be on his or her record so that one day, the fees for those services can be re-payed?

The best example to show the value of a financial accountability notion being built into all government systems is the case of a lottery winner. Let's say she has been on government care and cash all her life. With no accountability system as the one we are proposing, even Uncle Sam would have no idea how much was spent on her care and feeding before she won the lottery.

How many dollars or in-kind welfare are received?

And so, when their ship comes in, even lottery winners know there is no need to pay back anything to the fine taxpayers who helped get them through the tough times in their lives. They know that the taxpayers did not keep track of anything, and there is never a need to pay anything back... Nothing.... Ever...per year or per ever?

You may have read about cases in which the converse is true however. What about a massive lottery winner, who continues to collect their government benefits and they never look back and they never pay anything back. Worse than that, they never think of telling the government to shut off their benefits because they are now OK!

Intrinsically, we all know this is wrong. However, I would never suggest that when a positive life changing event occurs that government step in and ruin the parade completely. Does the lottery win make the new millionaire an elite? Possibly, but so what? I see no problem in raining on say half of the parade for big lottery winners, who owe society for their personal care over many years. But not all!

Why should a future lottery winner at a minimum not have to pay back what he or she has received in benefits over the years? They will not be inclined to ever pay them back unless we, the givers keep track of our "gifts." Lottery winners are not the only ones who should pay back.

Is everything free?

All receivers should pay back something for what they received when they needed help the most. Why should they not want to? Government until today has implicitly told them it was a gift from their neighborhood politician. Hopefully, the President Trump Administration will correct this misimpression of justice.

By the way, to repeat, in this instance, I would limit the government's take to 50% of lottery winnings to pay back lifestyles paid by taxpayers even if the winner owed more. There is a reason for this.

Who would ever play the lottery, theoretically beneficial to poor Americans, if all the proceeds went to our wasteful government officials?

Additionally, people recovering from disabilities that put them on the dole. As they recover, and as their fortunes change, it would not be bad for them to be asked to pay back something—let's say on a yearly basis to ease the strain on taxpayers. I think if we only asked them by name, they would help the rest of the unfortunate. Of course, it is vital to have all names and records.

So, the bottom line is that an Accountability database whatever you choose to label it, should be built to track unpaid taxes, expenses—all debts owed in the Resident Visa Holder process. It does not matter if it was OK or not OK debt; earned or unearned; paid or unpaid. The day has come for debts to the people to be repaid.

The Resident Visa renewal on-site appearance can be used to assure that all former interloper debt is paid. The fee each year must be paid and not put on account. There are no excuses. Either the visa holder makes full payment or an approved partial payment of their Accountability balance, or they would be put on a USCIS approved payment plan. Or, of course, there is always voluntary deportation.

If former interlopers refuse to pay what the agents think is a proper amount or if they refuse to pay anything at all towards their fines, and back taxes, they are candidates for a deportation that must happen. It must be a risky proposition for the former interloper in order to assure their compliance and payment. – Of course, payments can be made as small as necessary to assure that something is paid every year.

Additional charges may be assessed by the interviewers based on the behavior of the interviewee.

For example, if the aspirant gives a hard-working USCIS agent or a stand-in from the Post Office a hard time when calculating debt, taxes, etc., Why should that not cost the aspirant an extra fine?

The cost for any extra interview time should be paid by the aspirant at an appropriate cost rate. The computer program may advise the interviewer that an additional fee needs to be collected right then and there.

In every instance in which an aspirant or a Resident Visa holder indiscriminately and inappropriately takes more interviewer time than deemed appropriate, their Accountability record should absorb an extra charge or they should pay the charge immediately at the discretion of the agent.

These records would be kept to assuring payback over time. And, so, in the long run, there are no costs to the US taxpayer.

The database records of registrants should "never" be deleted. I would think that a record deletion should need proof of death for at least 50 years in the grave. The US objective is to collect for all debts from the debtor or the beneficiary of the debts.

Taxpayers want a nice fair deal for interlopers that does not involve the taxpayer having to pay a dime. That is the purpose of this book. If Resident Visa status individuals want to take advantage of American taxpayers in ways not shown in this book, this scribe suggests the Resident Visa holder pays the toll and then some.

Chapter 19 Summary and Conclusions

The Resident Visa Plan and Millions of Illegal Foreign Nationals

This is the solution for all of the 60 million illegal residents in America today. The Resident Visa Plan takes interlopers out of the shadows and makes Americans the citizen kings and citizen queens of our own country once again. It defines terms under which Americans gain by accepting illegal interlopers into a special visa program. For this, they pay for a passport and a visa, and each year, they pay an annual visa renewal fee.

Having a Resident Visa would take a former illegal alien out of the shadows and legalize them so they can lead a normal life in normal neighborhoods in the United States. For well-behaved, approved Resident Visa Holders, this provides a mechanism where they can stay in America for life as temporary residents one year at a time. The implementation of this plan makes the US a sovereign country again, never again to be attacked by border jumpers and visa overstayers.

This is not amnesty; but it is legalization. The Resident Visa Holders will pay a fine and pay back some of the debt they owe from taking benefits for years from the US welfare system. It is the best approach to deal with 60 million illegal foreign nationals living in the US. Today, they live clandestine lives in shadows and sanctuary cities in our country.

Temporary Visa Holders can keep their current jobs but they never get to vote in any election; are not eligible for benefits; never become citizens; and they never get hired for a job before an American citizen.

In essence this plan eliminates the shadows as well as the need for sanctuary cities. It eliminates all freebies as well as illegal voting. It provides job priority for Americans instead of interlopers. It grants no path to citizenship but it permits resident visa holders to go back to their home country to sign up for citizenship according to their country's rules. At the same time, it brings the cost of supporting illegal foreign nationals to zero. In fact, after this program is implemented there will be no more illegal foreign nationals.

Deportations will be minimized but will occur as an enforcement mechanism and for interlopers who come after this program is commenced. Those illegal interlopers who choose not to gain a Resident Visa or who are not approved after vetting, will be offered a Pay-to-Go option which will provide travel expenses and a large stipend to leave the country and return home.

A look at the numbers shows that the cost to Americans is approaching $1Trillion in terms of welfare, Job-loss, and wage depression. This plan solves all of that. It makes big financial sense for America; helps America keep its unique identity, and it puts Americans on top again where we belong.

Made in the USA
Monee, IL
04 November 2026

67385047R00105